Southea

Travel Guide 2023

Discover the Enchanting Wonders of Southeast Asia, A Comprehensive Travel Guide for 2023

Melissa Martino

Copyright © 2023 Melissa Martino

All rights reserved. No part of this book may be reproduced, stored in a retrieval system, or transmitted in any form or by any means, electronic, mechanical, photocopying, recording, scanning or otherwise, without the prior writing permission of the copyright owner.

Table of Contents

Table of Contents	**3**
Introduction	**6**
Map of Southeast Asia	**14**
Chapter One	**15**
What is Southeast Asia, exactly?	15
Itinerary	19
DAY 1	19
DAY 2	20
DAY 3	21
DAY 4	22
DAY 5	23
DAY 6	24
Chapter Two	**27**
Planning Your Trip	27
Best Time to Visit Southeast Asia	27
A MONTHLY GUIDE TO TRAVELING TO SOUTHEAST ASIA	28
Visa Requirements	30
Beaches	33
Travel Insurance	36
Budgeting and Money Matters	41
Safety Tips and Precautions	44
Chapter Three	**48**
Getting to Southeast Asia	48
Air Travel	48
Overland Travel	49
Local Transportation	50

Budget airlines	50
Chapter Four	**54**
Navigating Southeast Asia	54
Transportation Systems	54
Language and Communication	57
Currency and Exchange	61
Accommodation Options	64
Chapter Five	**69**
Exploring Southeast Asia	69
Overview of the Countries	69
Thailand	69
Map of Indonesia	74
Indonesia	75
Map of Vietnam	80
Vietnam	81
Map of Malaysia	87
Malaysia	88
Map of Philippines	95
Philippines	96
Map of Singapore	103
Singapore	104
Map of Cambodia	110
Cambodia	111
Map of Laos	116
Laos	117
Map of Burma	121
Burma	122
Off the Beaten Path Destinations	126
Chapter Six	**131**

Food and cuisine	131
Local Favorites	140
A Street Food Guide	143
Vegetarian and Vegan Options	146
Dining Etiquette	149
Chapter Seven	**154**
Cultural Insights	154
History and Heritage	154
Religion and Beliefs	156
Festivals and Celebrations	159
Chapter Eight	**170**
Practical Information	170
Health and Safety	170
Money-saving Tips	173
Connectivity and the Internet	177
Essential Phrases	180
Conclusion	**185**
Recommended Reading	185
Index	188

Introduction

I once visited Southeast Asia, hoping to see the region's rich cultural diversity and stunning natural beauty. I had no idea my voyage would be a fantastic experience that would forever change my heart.

Bangkok, Thailand, a bustling city, was where my journey began. The lively streets' colorful tuk-tuks and fragrant food carts instantly drew my attention. Ancient temples coexisted peacefully with modern skyscrapers in the world. I suddenly represented the region's distinctive blend of history and growth.

Following my wanderlust, I entered the historic city of Ayutthaya and gawked at the stunning temple and palace ruins that still stood there. I couldn't help but feel a strong connection to the past and the people who had thrived in this lovely site as I took in the history and beauty of this UNESCO World Heritage Site.

I left Thailand and landed in Bali, Indonesia's beautiful beach. My breath was taken away by the island's breathtaking natural beauty, which included its emerald-green rice terraces and stunning beaches. I savored the locals' warm hospitality as they shared their traditional dances, exquisite craftsmanship, and delectable feasts with me. I found solace in the peace of Ubud, where I studied Balinese philosophy and performed yoga among gorgeous tropical trees.

I continued my journey by flying to Vietnam, where she enjoyed the chaotic allure of Hanoi's Old Quarter. The crowded markets offered a fascinating tapestry of sights, sounds, and feelings as vendors offered colorful handicrafts and aromatic street food. I began a magnificent journey around Halong Bay's breathtaking limestone karsts, marveling at nature's incredible artistic talent in every rock structure and brilliantly green water. I visited the historic temple of Angkor Wat in Cambodia while traveling around Southeast Asia. I was filled with awe and admiration for human civilization's ingenuity as I gazed at the enormous stone monuments that were painstakingly engraved with historical narratives.

On the last leg of the trip, I visited Phuket, Thailand's stunning beaches. The clear waters, swaying palm trees, and gentle sea breeze provided the perfect environment for reflection and repose. I immersed myself in the community's culture, discovering the distinctive customs and traditions of the Thai people. I even got to see a traditional Thai boxing match, which displayed skill, discipline, and strength.

I realized my journey had been more than just a series of stops as I sadly said farewell to Southeast Asia. It had been a life-changing event that broadened my horizons, deepened my understanding of other people's cultures, and sparked a deep reverence for the world's natural splendor.

Southeast Asia had me under its spell, leaving me with memories that would live on in my heart for a long time. My sense of curiosity had been sparked by the region's warmth, vibrant colors, and rich heritage, which led me to embrace new ideas and appreciate the amazing diversity of our planet.

Ultimately, my journey to Southeast Asia had been more than just a research expedition; it had also been a very moving experience that ignited a lifelong passion for exploration, cross-cultural interaction, and the innate beauty that resides inside every aspect of our planet.

Welcome, from the "Southeast Asia Travel Guide 2023"! This comprehensive guide is intended to be your travel companion as you embark on an unforgettable journey around Southeast Asia's beautiful and diverse region. This book is intended to provide accurate and up-to-date information, insider advice, and inspired ideas to make your travel experience utterly unique, whether you are a seasoned traveler or visiting this part of the world for the first time.

A spellbinding blend of ancient customs, breathtaking landscapes, vibrant cultures, and delectable cuisine can be found across Southeast Asia. This region has many intriguing sights just waiting to be discovered, from the chaotic streets of Bangkok to the serene beaches of Bali, from the lush forests of Borneo to the magnificent temples of Angkor Wat.

To help you manage the unique quirks of each Southeast Asian country, we have painstakingly gathered a range of information in this book. Comprehensive chapters on well-known tourist locations, including Thailand, Vietnam, Cambodia, Malaysia, Indonesia, and the Philippines, may be found here, along with chapters on lesser-known gems that deserve your attention.

Our team of seasoned travel writers and regional authorities has gone above and beyond to ensure that the information provided in this book is accurate and representative of the most recent trends and developments. To help you make the most of your vacation to Southeast Asia, we've included useful advice on transportation, lodging, cultural customs, and essential travel tips.

Beyond the necessities, we work to pique your sense of exploration and curiosity. Explore hidden old sites in the forest, get lost in crowded street markets, savor the delicacies of local cuisine, stroll through remote mountain scenery, and interact with the friendly locals who will undoubtedly make a lasting impression on your vacation.

This travel guide is your key to discovering Southeast Asia's wonders, whether you're looking for a serene spiritual retreat in Bali, an exhilarating adventure in the Borneo jungles, a cultural immersion in the ancient temples of Myanmar, or a beach paradise in the unspoiled islands of Thailand.

The pages of this book will provide a vivid image of Southeast Asia's rich history, natural beauty, diverse cultures, and unforgettable experiences. We invite you to come along on this amazing adventure with us. As you explore Southeast Asia's hidden beauties, get ready to be enveloped in a kaleidoscope of hues, aromas, and feelings.

Pack your bags, satisfy your curiosity, and allow the "Southeast Asia Travel Guide 2023" to be your dependable travel companion on this amazing exploration journey. Best regards!

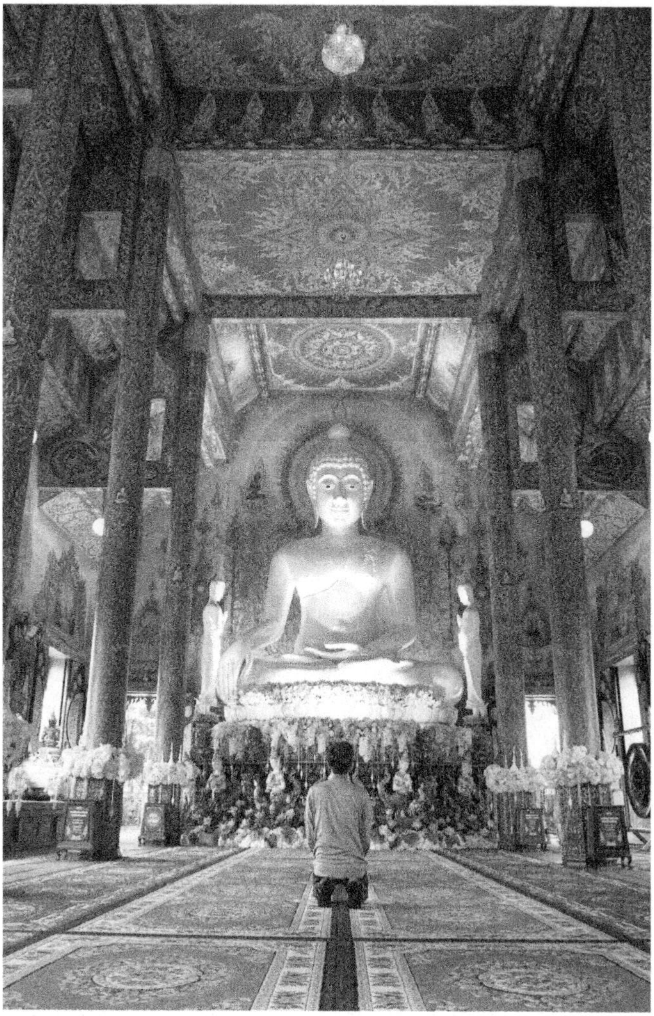

Map of Southeast Asia

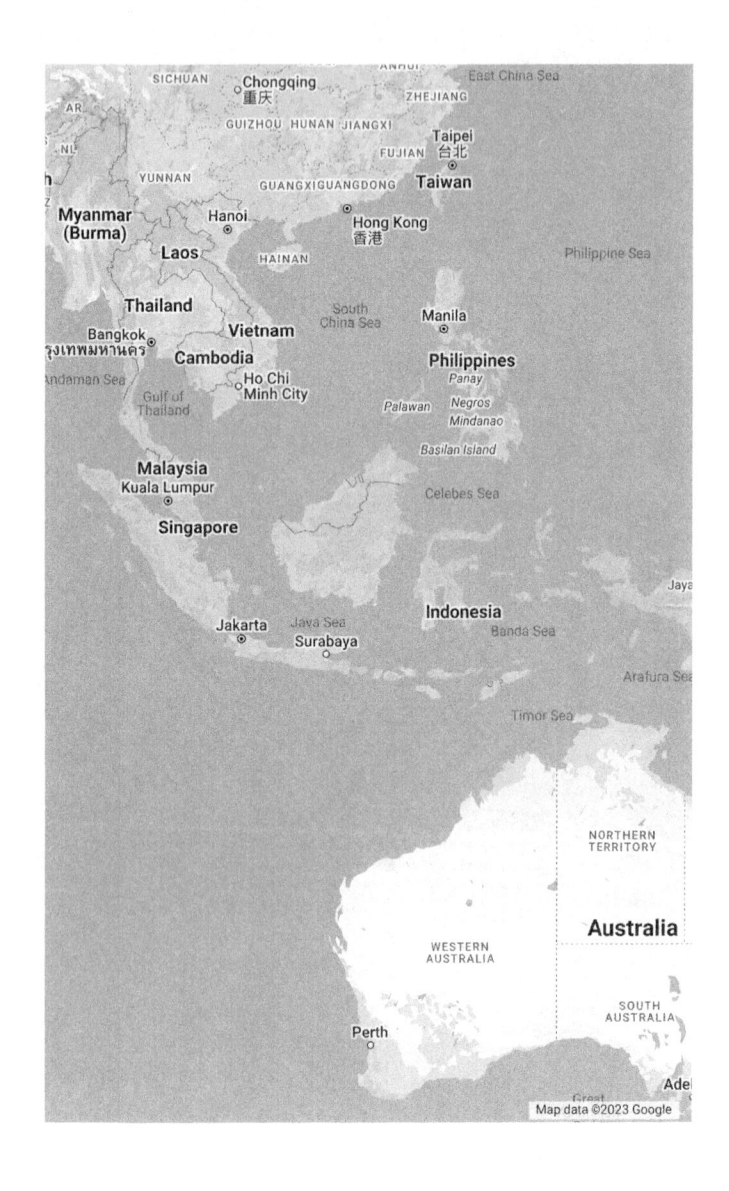

Chapter One

What is Southeast Asia, exactly?

Southeast Asia's subregion is located in the southeast of the Asian continent. This diverse and culturally rich region comprises Brunei, Cambodia, Indonesia, Laos, Malaysia, Myanmar (Burma), the Philippines, Singapore, Thailand, Timor-Leste, and Vietnam.

Southeast Asia is connected to the Asian peninsula through landmasses and the Eurasian Plate, and it is physically limited to the east by the Pacific Ocean and to the south by the Indian Ocean. More than 655 million people live in about 4.5 million square kilometers.

The region's geography is diverse, with long beaches, mountain ranges, and lush rainforests among its features. Due to its abundant natural resources, which include oil, natural gas, minerals, and biodiversity, Southeast Asia is significant commercially.

Southeast Asia's culture comprises a diverse tapestry of ethnicities, languages, religions, and traditions. The most common religions are Islam, Buddhism, Christianity, Hinduism, and other indigenous beliefs. The architecture, the arts, the festivals, and the daily lives of the local populace have all been significantly influenced by this religious diversity.

The history of Southeast Asia is convoluted, influenced by native civilizations, trade routes, colonization, and aspirations for liberation. Many cultures have left behind long legacies in terms of architecture, art, and cultural heritage, including the Khmer Empire, the Majapahit Empire, and the Srivijaya Empire.

During the colonial era, European nations occupied Southeast Asia, including the British, Dutch, French, and Spanish. After World War II, the region saw a wave of decolonization that led to the establishment of independent nations.

Southeast Asia is a region with a thriving economy and is expanding swiftly. It benefits from trade, investment, and tourism with firms in various sectors, from manufacturing and agriculture to technology and services. The ASEAN organization, established in 1967, promotes political stability, economic integration, and regional cooperation among its member nations.

Many Southeast Asian countries' economies greatly benefit from tourism, which draws travelers to the region's stunning landscapes, ancient temples, vibrant cities, and distinctive cultural experiences. Popular tourist destinations include the beaches of Thailand, Angkor Wat in Cambodia, Ha Long Bay in Vietnam, and Bali in Indonesia.

To sum up, Southeast Asia is an intriguing and diverse Asian subregion known for its stunning natural beauty, rich cultural heritage, and promising future. It is an interesting subject for researchers interested in exploring the nuances of this vibrant region due to its unique blend of traditions, beliefs, and landscapes.

Itinerary

DAY 1

MORNING
Start your day by seeing Penang Bridge, which connects Penang Island to the mainland and is one of Southeast Asia's longest bridges. To experience breathtaking views of the area, drive or walk over the bridge.

AFTERNOON
Discover the breathtaking Koh Haa islands, which are located off the Thai coast. Discover the vibrant marine life and coral reefs by snorkeling or diving in the clear waters.

EVENING
Visit Okinawa World, a theme park in Japan that honors the natural beauty, culture, and history of Okinawa. Explore the gardens, traditional homes, and limestone tunnels

before attending an Okinawan dance performance.

DAY 2

MORNING

You may immerse yourself in Okinawa's rich history at Ryukyu Mura, an outdoor museum replicating a typical Okinawan village. Learn about the unique customs, architecture, and culture of the Ryukyu Kingdom.

AFTERNOON

Discover Mu Ko Lanta National Park in Thailand, which contains several islands and stunning beaches. Go snorkeling, take a boat tour of the islands, or unwind on the beautiful beaches.

EVENING

Discover the rich marine life, which includes whale sharks, manta rays, and tropical fish, at

Okinawa Churaumi Aquarium, one of the largest aquariums in the world.

DAY 3

MORNING
Visit Ho Chi Minh City from a different perspective by cruising the Saigon River in Vietnam. Discover the history and culture of the Mekong Delta by visiting its cities and floating markets.

AFTERNOON
On Thailand's Koh Tao Island, unwind on the white sands of Aow Leuk Beach. Swim, snorkel, or sunbathe and relax in the serene environment.

EVENING
One of the largest Buddhist temples in Southeast Asia is Kek Lok Si Temple in Penang, Malaysia. Explore the temple complex, see the

magnificent design, and take in the expansive views of the area.

DAY 4

MORNING
On Koh Mook Island in Thailand, explore the Emerald Cave. Swim down a narrow channel to reach a hidden beach bordered by limestone cliffs, offering a lovely and secluded haven.

AFTERNOON
Visit Thailand's beautiful Koh Kradan island, known for its coral reefs, pristine waters, and white sand beaches. Other activities include snorkeling, lying on the beach, and soaking up the sun.

EVENING
At Johor Bahru's LEGOLAND Malaysia, have fun all day. Discover the theme park, take in

the thrilling activities, and be amazed by the incredible LEGO creations.

DAY 5

MORNING

Visit the little Thai island of Nang Yuan, which is close to Koh Tao, by boat. Take time to unwind on the stunning beaches, snorkel in the calm waters, or go to the viewpoint for expansive views.

AFTERNOON

To learn more about Penang, Malaysia's history and culture, visit the Penang State Museum and Art Gallery. Visit the exhibitions and galleries to see the works of traditional art, antiquities, and records from history.

EVENING

At Laser Battle in Malaysia, you may enjoy a game of laser tag with your loved ones. Test your strategic abilities in this engaging game filled with action.

DAY 6

MORNING

Visit Malaysia's Sultan Abu Bakar State Mosque, a breathtaking building renowned for its exquisite design and sweeping vistas of Johor Bahru. Discover the mosque's importance in Islamic culture by exploring the mosque's grounds.

AFTERNOON

Johor Bahru, Malaysia's Angry Birds Activity Park, is a fun day spot. Enjoy various interactive Angry Birds-themed games, rides, and other attractions.

EVENING

Learn about Thomas Town Puteri Harbour, an indoor park with a Johor Bahru theme that offers activities based on popular children's personalities like Bob the Builder and Thomas the Tank Engine.

Chapter Two

Planning Your Trip

Best Time to Visit Southeast Asia

November through February are the best for travel to Southeast Asia. With average temperatures of about 30°C, the area has drier, less humid, and slightly colder weather. But for the nights, bring a thick jacket. Southeast Asia's rainy season, which lasts from June to October, causes gorgeous paddy fields in Cambodia and Vietnam and floods in the Mekong Delta. The monsoon season is sometimes the most reasonable time to visit Southeast Asia for flights and hotels, provided you don't mind a little rain.

A MONTHLY GUIDE TO TRAVELING TO SOUTHEAST ASIA

Southeast Asia has two distinct seasons: the dry season, which lasts from December to April, and the rainy season, which lasts from May to October or November. Regardless of when you intend to visit, you will almost certainly find pleasant weather someplace since it is a big territory with various microclimates.

As the dry season ends in March, temperatures start to climb. They may approach 40°C in certain places with significant humidity in April. At this time of year, the highlands are a welcome retreat.

Several crucial industries have difficulties during the rainy season. Travel is challenging due to flooding in the Mekong Delta. The Andaman Coast of Thailand has the most rainfall, and high waves may make it difficult for boats to get to places like Bamboo Island near Kep. Though there are fewer tourists and less rain at this time of year in the Gulf of

Thailand, certain islands, like Koh Samet, have lovely microclimates. In September and October, more rain is anticipated.

Tropical cyclones may form in coastal regions during the rainy season; if you plan to travel during this period, pay attention to weather forecasts.

Visit the Con Dao Archipelago in Vietnam in July, August, or the first part of September to watch turtles laying their eggs.

The biggest New Year's celebration in Vietnam is called Tet. It takes place on the same day as Chinese New Year, in late January or early February. Avoid this time of year if you don't want to participate since there will be many people, crowded public transportation, and many attractions closing for up to a week.

Kho Pha Ngan has a filthy tourist swarm throughout the whole year, but once a month, particularly in January, it becomes even worse as up to 30,000 hedonists arrive just in time for the Full Moon Party. This event has no standard components since it was developed for and by Westerners. It's advised to avoid "Half Moon Parties" for guests arriving later in the lunar cycle since lodging is completely booked, music plays nonstop, and the beach is littered with broken glass and burning cigarettes.

Visa Requirements

You may need a visa depending on the country you wish to visit in Southeast Asia. While many Southeast Asian nations allow visitors from certain nations entry without a permit or with a visa upon arrival, others need a ticket in advance.

Below is a summary of the visa requirements for many significant Southeast Asian countries:

Thailand: Citizens of several countries, including the US, Canada, and most EU states, do not need a visa to enter Thailand and remain there for up to 30 days. A tourist visa or a non-immigrant visa may be required for longer journeys.

Vietnam: Most travelers must get a visa in advance. For a limited time, some nationals, including those of the United Kingdom, France, Germany, Spain, Italy, and other ASEAN nations, may visit Vietnam without a visa. Based on nationality, the length of the visa-free stay varies.

Indonesia: Without a visa, visitors from more than 169 nations may travel to Indonesia and remain for up to 30 days. The Visa Exemption for Short Visits policy governs this.

Malaysia: For stays of up to 90 days, visitors from several nations, including the US, Canada, the UK, Australia, and most European countries, are not needed to get a visa. However, the period of stay may differ based on nationality.

Singapore: Depending on nationality, citizens of different countries may enter without a visa for 30 to 90 days. However, a permit is required ahead of time for certain nations.

Philippines: For stays of up to 30 days, citizens of several nations—including the

United States, Canada, the United Kingdom, Australia, and most European countries—do not need a visa. Obtaining a permit may be necessary for longer visits.

Cambodia: At major airports and land border crossings, most visitors from other nations may get a visa for Cambodia upon arrival. Using the ticket is valid for 30 days.

Laos: Most nations, including those from the United States, Canada, the United Kingdom, Australia, and most of Europe, may get a visa for Laos upon arrival at the country's main airports and land border crossings. Using the ticket is valid for 30 days.

Myanmar (Burma): Most travelers to Myanmar (Burma) must get a visa in advance. There are many variations of tickets, including tourist and business visas. Contact the Myanmar embassy or consulate closest to you for the latest recent details.

The most exact and current information on visa requirements, application processes, and any other entry restrictions should always be obtained from the embassy or consulate of the country you plan to visit. It is crucial to remember that visa rules may vary.

Beaches

Southeast Asia is home to some of the most stunning beaches on earth.
You can't go wrong with any of the stunning nations in Southeast Asia if you choose to go there. The stunning beaches of Southeast Asia are wonderful travel destinations.

Here are a few of Southeast Asia's most stunning beaches that you should visit:

El Nido, Philippines: El Nido is a tropical haven situated on the Philippine island of Palawan. Due to its colorful flora and animals, El Nido, which means "the nest," is one of the nation's most diversified ecosystems. 50 white sand beaches, 5 distinct kinds of forests, 3 main marine ecosystems, and 813 fish species can be found in the province.

El Nido is a fantastic destination if you wish to go from one beach to the next. Simizu Island, Bacuit Bay, and Seven Commandos Beach are more local attractions.

El Nido: where various experiences await you if you wish to have a pleasant trip.

Ngapali Beach in Myanmar may be the ideal location if you're looking for a more relaxing vacation. The picturesque island in Myanmar is among the most well-liked travel locations there.

Ngapali Beach Myanmar: Due in part to stringent regulations prohibiting motorized vehicles in the region, Ngapali Beach is renowned for its calm and picturesque surroundings.

Even though there aren't many things to do on the island, Ngapali Beach is a great place to unwind and lose weight.

Komodo Island in Indonesia: is a center of great activities simply waiting to be found, as indicated by its name alone. The Komodo Dragon, which bears the island's name, is the biggest lizard in the world and lives on Komodo Island.

To witness one of nature's most spectacular beasts, go to Komodo Island. There are numerous more stunning places in this area. One of only seven "pink beaches" worldwide is located on Komodo Island. White and red sand are combined to create pink sand.

Visit Jaco Island in East Timor: the isolation and peace there will give you a fresh feeling of enthusiasm. East Timor's Jaco Island is uninhabited.

Camping or staying on the island for a lengthy period of time is challenging. By hiring a native to transport you, you may still get to the island and take in its natural beauty.

An Bang, Vietnam: Nature seems much more attractive when it lacks artificial trash. A Bang, the diligent residents who labor ceaselessly to maintain the sandy beaches' beauty adhere to this attitude.

You may unwind, relax, and eat a fresh mango while enjoying the stunning scenery along the shore.

Travel Insurance

Every traveler to this unique and exciting area should have travel insurance for Southeast Asia. Southeast Asia attracts tourists from all over the globe because of its magnificent natural beauty, rich cultural history, and wide variety of engaging activities. Unexpected occurrences like accidents, sickness, trip cancellations, or missing things may cause vacation plans to fall through and incur hefty financial obligations. Travel insurance offers protection and peace of mind by shielding travelers from unforeseen circumstances.

Coverage and coverage: Travel insurance plans for Southeast Asia often provide various coverage options customized to the unique requirements of travelers to this area. Examples of typical travel insurance coverage areas include the following:

Medical Expenses: Travel insurance covers medical costs incurred while traveling due to illnesses or accidents. All medical expenses, including hospitalization, emergency care, physician fees, and prescription drugs, are covered.

Emergency Evacuation: Travel insurance ensures that the costs are paid in the event of a medical emergency requiring an urgent evacuation or repatriation to one's home country. Such evacuation may be necessary in Southeast Asia's rural or impoverished regions due to the lack of medical treatment.

Travel insurance reimburses you for non-refundable costs like airline tickets, hotel reservations, and tour bookings if your trip to Southeast Asia is canceled or cut short due to unforeseeable events such as medical problems, calamities, or political instability.

Travel insurance reimburses consumers for the loss, theft, or damage to their luggage or other personal possessions in case of a baggage delay or failure. Additionally, it pays for any items that must be bought due to the delayed luggage.

Personal Liability: Travel insurance will pay for any necessary legal expenses and compensation claims if you accidentally harm someone or damage their property while on vacation.

Services for travel assistance: Many travel insurance plans include access to helplines, translation services, travel counseling, and cooperation with regional authorities or healthcare facilities.

Considerations for Southeast Asia: It's crucial to remember the following things when acquiring travel insurance for Southeast Asia.

Medical Coverage: Because healthcare prices vary widely across nations, be sure that your insurance plan offers enough coverage for medical charges in Southeast Asia. It is advisable to get emergency medical evacuation insurance since it can be required in remote or undeveloped places.

Adventure Activities: Southeast Asia provides a wide variety of adventure activities, including motorcycle tours, trekking, and scuba diving. See whether your insurance policy covers these activities or if you need to get extra coverage.

Pre-existing conditions: Inform the insurance provider of any existing medical issues before acquiring a policy since certain policies may have restrictions or exclusions for such ailments.

Consider both the flexibility of your insurance coverage and the duration of your trip. Be sure your insurance covers this if you want to prolong your stay or make several travels throughout Southeast Asia.

Budgeting and Money Matters

With a wide range of accommodations, dining options, and activities, Southeast Asia is an affordable holiday location. Here are some suggestions on how to set a budget for your Southeast Asian vacation:

Set a budget: Setting a budget is the first stage in arranging a trip. It can help you stay on track and avoid paying too much.

Research accommodation: Lodging is one of the biggest expenses while traveling to Southeast Asia. Numerous lodging options are available, ranging from pricey hostels to opulent hotels. Find accommodations that fit your needs and your budget by doing some research.

Eat local food: Eating regional food is a great way to save costs when traveling in Southeast Asia—typically affordable and delicious street cuisine. You could also come across inexpensive restaurants serving regional cuisine.

Do free activities: Southeast Asia offers a wealth of free activities. Explore temples, stroll through markets, or observe people. Free activities are also available, including cycling, hiking, and visiting local towns.

Be prepared to bargain: haggling is a way of life in Southeast Asia. Never hesitate to barter for trinkets, taxi rides, and other goods and services.

Here are some approximate travel spending ranges for Southeast Asia:

Budget backpacker: $35 to $40 per day
Traveler in the middle: $50 to $60 per day
Traveler in luxury: $100+ daily
These are only estimates, and your actual costs may change depending on how you like to holiday and the activities you choose. These budgets could give you a good place to start when planning your trip.

Here are some additional tips for budgeting and money matters in Southeast Asia:

Bring some cash with you: Although credit cards are often accepted across Southeast Asia, carrying some cash with you is a good idea, especially if you want to go to remote areas.

Exchange your money at a local bank or currency exchange: Change your currency at a nearby bank or exchange house: At a local bank or currency exchange, you'll get a better exchange rate than you would at the airport.

Be aware of ATM fees: Be cautious of ATM fees since they might be costly in Southeast Asia. Try to use ATMs that don't charge a fee.

Please keep track of your spending: It's simple to overspend when traveling, so keeping tabs on your spending is essential. Numerous tools are available to help you keep track of your spending.

If you research and plan, creating a budget for a trip to Southeast Asia may be easy. You may save money and have a great time on your trip by heeding these suggestions.

Safety Tips and Precautions

Southeast Asia is a beautiful, diverse region with something for everyone. Before traveling, you must be informed of the safety issues. To keep you safe when traveling in Southeast Asia, consider the following safety tips and precautions:

Be aware of your surroundings: This is especially important in crowded places like marketplaces, temples, and tourist attractions. Keep your belongings close by and watch out for anybody following you.

Don't flash your valuables: Keep your valuables hidden, including cash, jewelry, and gadgets. Put your valuables in a safe place, like a money belt or a hotel secure, if you must carry them.

Be careful when using public transportation: Pickpocketing is a common occurrence on public transit, so keep your belongings close at hand. Keep your bags in the overhead bins or under your seat if traveling by bus or train.

Be aware of scams: Scams are prevalent throughout Southeast Asia, and many of them prey on tourists. The following are some scams that happen frequently:

The "accidental" bump: A con artist will run into you and then say they broke their phone or other valuables. They will then demand payment from you to make up for the damage.

The "fake" police officer: A con artist will approach you and pose as a policeman. After then, they will accuse you of committing a crime and demand you pay a fine.

The "bargaining scam": involves a con artist taking you to a shop and claiming low prices. The merchant will, however, forbid you from leaving until you pay a far higher price when you try to do so.

Be careful what you eat and drink: Eat and drink cautiously since tap water in Southeast Asia is unsafe to consume. Drinking bottled or heated water should be done with caution. Steer clear of shellfish, fish, and uncooked or undercooked meat.

Get immunized: Travelers to Southeast Asia are urged to get a variety of immunizations. These include typhoid, hepatitis A, and yellow fever vaccines.

Get vaccinated: Purchase travel insurance to help you pay for unexpected expenses like medical bills, lost luggage, and trip cancellation.

Buy travel insurance: By adhering to these safety recommendations, you may ensure a safe and enjoyable trip to Southeast Asia.

Here are some additional tips:
- Learn a few basic words and phrases in the native tongue. It will facilitate communication and avoid misunderstandings with the populace.

- Respect the traditions and practices of the community. By doing this, you may avoid offending anybody and enjoy your trip more.
- Have a wonderful time! Southeast Asia is a beautiful, fascinating region with plenty to offer. Take time to unwind, have fun, and enjoy your holiday.

Chapter Three

Getting to Southeast Asia

Southeast Asia offers a rich and diverse experience with its stunning landscapes, intriguing civilizations, and unique traditions. To ensure that your vacation to Southeast Asia is as simple and enjoyable as possible, here are some of the best ways to go there:

Air Travel

The most common and convenient way to travel to Southeast Asia is via air. Direct flights from several international carriers are available to popular regional locations, including Bangkok, Singapore, Kuala Lumpur, and Ho Chi Minh City. By bringing you quickly and efficiently to your destination, air travel allows you to save time and energy.

Plan Your Itinerary: Southeast Asia is home to several countries, each with unique attractions. Ensure your agenda is well-planned before you go to maximize your time and investigate the topics that interest you most. Consider the duration of your trip, visa requirements, and the sights you wish to visit in each country.

Overland Travel

Consider including overland travel in Southeast Asia in your itinerary. Thanks to the region's well-connected transportation networks, you can rapidly commute between countries. Buses, trains, and boats are common modes of transit that provide stunning views and opportunities for interaction with locals. Take a boat from Vietnam to Cambodia or a rail from Thailand to Malaysia, for instance.

Local Transportation

To immerse yourself in the local culture and taste Southeast Asia's essence, investigate local transportation options within each country.

Tuk-tuks, motorbike taxis, and cyclos are common modes of transportation in many cities. In rural areas, you can encounter rickshaws or horse-drawn carriages as transportation. When using these forms of transportation, always agree on the price in advance and proceed with prudence.

Budget airlines

Low-cost carriers provide convenient local and international travel options for Southeast Asia. Thanks to airlines like AirAsia, Jetstar Asia, and Lion Air, you can travel around the region at a reasonable price. However, confirm any baggage restrictions and additional fees before making a reservation.

Island hopping: Southeast Asia has some of the world's most exquisite tropical islands. Think of island-hopping to visit the Phi Phi Islands in Thailand, Bali and the Gili Islands in Indonesia, or Palawan in the Philippines. Using ferries, speedboats, and planned visits makes island hopping simpler and more enjoyable.

Local Knowledge and Guides: Organizing tours or hiring local guides may greatly enhance your Southeast Asia travel experience. They provide helpful information, assist you in overcoming language barriers, and ensure you don't miss out on any undiscovered gems. Additionally, local guides may offer ideas for real, local experiences and safety tips.

Research Local Customs and Etiquette: Each nation in Southeast Asia has its own social mores and cultural traditions. Before your trip, research and learn about regional customs and etiquette. Make interactions with locals more enjoyable and meaningful by demonstrating respect and preventing inadvertent cultural faux pas.

Stay Hydrated and Practice Good Hygiene: Southeast Asia has a tropical climate, so being hydrated is crucial, especially on hot, muggy days. Keep hydrated by carrying a bottle of water. Also, practice good hygiene by washing your hands often, especially before meals, to prevent health hazards.

Pack Accordingly: Last, pack sensibly for your trip to Southeast Asia. Consider the local climatic conditions, scheduled activities, and cultural sensitivity. You should pack breathable, light clothing, comfortable shoes, insect repellant, sunscreen, and a travel adapter.

You'll be ready to go on an incredible trip across the fascinating countries of Southeast Asia by paying attention to these recommendations. Enjoy yourself and become fully involved in your travels.

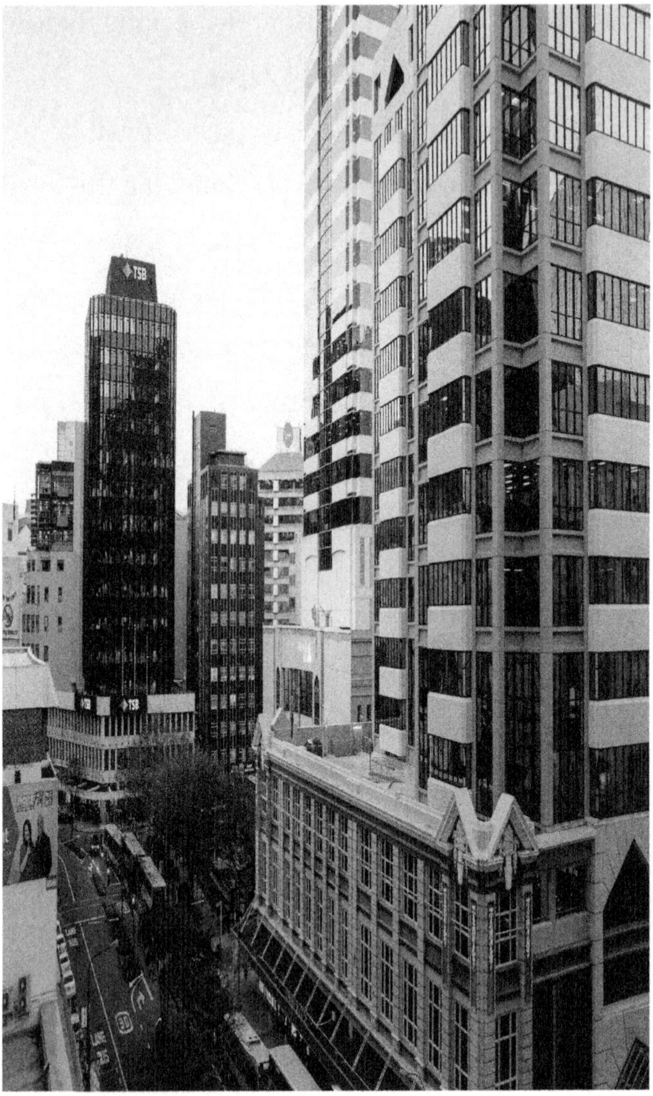
TSB

Chapter Four

Navigating Southeast Asia

Transportation Systems

Southeast Asia's transportation systems include a variety of modern and ancient modes of transportation. The most typical forms of transportation are:

Road transport: For passenger and freight traffic, roads are Southeast Asia's primary mode of transportation. Southeast Asia has a sizable road system is constantly being expanded and improved.

Rail travel: Although less common than road travel in Southeast Asia, rail travel is an important mode of transportation in several nations, including Thailand and Indonesia.

Air transport: Air travel is the fastest and most practical way to cover long distances in Southeast Asia. Southeast Asia is home to several international airports and has a thriving local airline industry.

Water transport: In Southeast Asia, particularly for trade and business, water transportation is a key mode of transportation. Numerous rivers and canals are present in the region, and goods and people may be transported via these waterways.

Non-motorized transport: In many parts of Southeast Asia, non-motorized transit, such as walking, cycling, and rickshaws, is still a major mode of transportation. These environmentally friendly and cost-effective modes of transportation are usually the only ones available for getting about in rural areas.

Non-motorized transport in Southeast Asia

In addition to these traditional modes of transportation, there are also several new and emerging modes of transportation in Southeast Asia, such as:

Shared mobility services: In Southeast Asia, services like bike-sharing and ride-hailing are growing in popularity. These services provide a practical and affordable way to go about, and they are reducing traffic congestion.

High-speed rail: Southeast Asia is developing high-speed rail as a new mode of transportation. High-speed rail is expected to significantly impact the region's economy and tourism since it is a faster and more effective way to traverse long distances.

High-speed rail in Southeast Asia: Southeast Asia's transportation networks are expanding and getting more integrated constantly. As a result, the region is becoming more connected, and moving people and goods around is becoming easier.

Language and Communication

The many languages and communication methods used by the different ethnic groups and nations in Southeast Asia are among the region's distinctive linguistic features. I may provide a brief overview of several key languages and communication methods used often in Southeast Asia, even though it is difficult to cover the whole of this linguistic environment.

Malay/Indonesian: Malaysian and Indonesian are both countries that speak the Malay language, one of Southeast Asia's major dialects. Along with Singapore, Brunei, and parts of Thailand, it is widely spoken there. There are several dialects and variations of the Malay language spoken across the region, but Indonesian is the standardized version based on the Malay language.

Thai: The majority of people in Thailand speak Thai, which is the official language of the country. It features a unique script and is a member of the Tai-Kadai language family. That is a challenging language for non-native speakers because it is tonal, meaning that different tones may influence the meaning of words.

Vietnamese: A significant portion of the population speaks Vietnamese, the country of Vietnam's official language. It is a Mon-Khmer language with Chinese linguistic traces. The Quoc Ngu alphabet, established during the French colonial period, is used to write Vietnamese. It is a modified version of the Latin alphabet.

Burmese: The official language of Myanmar (Burma) is Burmese. It is a Sino-Tibetan language that uses an alphabet of its own, the "Burmese script" or "Myanmar script," developed from the previous Brahmi system. Distinct ethnic groups in Myanmar speak different varieties of the Burmese language.

Khmer: Most Cambodians speak Khmer, the country's official language. It has its script, formed from ancient Indian hands, and is a member of the Austroasiatic language family. Its intricate vowel system distinguishes non-tonal Khmer.

Tagalog: Filipino, the country's official language, is built based on one of the Philippines' main languages, Tagalog. It employs the Latin alphabet and is a member of the Austronesian language family. There are around 170 different languages spoken in the Philippines, with Cebuano, Ilocano, and Hiligaynon among the famous regional tongues.

Other languages: Javanese, Sundanese, Madurese, Balinese, Batak, and Iban, are spoken throughout Southeast Asia. These languages, often written in their scripts or writing systems, are spoken by several ethnic groups in the region.

It's important to remember that, in addition to these spoken languages, English is commonly used as a lingua franca across Southeast Asia, particularly in urban areas, tourist destinations, and business settings. In Southeast Asia, many people talk in several regional tongues or dialects based on their ethnic backgrounds and local communities.

Southeast Asia has a diverse language environment that reflects the region's rich cultural history and historical impacts from neighboring countries.

Currency and Exchange

Southeast Asia is home to several countries, each with its own currency and trade method. Following are some of the local cash and some essential details on currency exchange:

Thai Baht (THB): The official money of Thailand is the Thai Baht. It is symbolized by the letter " or the word "THB" Around the country, there are several locations to exchange money, including airports, hotels, and well-known tourist attractions.

Indonesian Rupiah (IDR): The Indonesian Rupiah (IDR) is the country's official currency; it is represented by the letters "Rp" or "IDR." Around the country, banks authorized money changers, and airports offered currency exchange services.

Malaysian Ringgit (MYR): The ringgit is the official currency of Malaysia, and it is represented by the letters "M.R" or "MYR" Currency exchange counters are available in

57

airports, shopping malls, and well-known tourist attractions in Malaysia.

Singapore Dollar (SGD): The Singapore Dollar, abbreviated as "S$" or "SGD," is the country of Singapore's official currency. Banks and retail establishments all around the country provide convenient access to currency exchange services.

Philippine Peso (PHP): The Philippine Peso, represented by the letters " or "PHP," is the nation of the Philippines' official unit of exchange. Banks, licensed money changers, and a few hotels offer nationwide currency exchange services.

Vietnamese Dong (VND): The Vietnamese Dong, sometimes known as "V.N.D." is the national currency of Vietnam. Banks, airports, and approved exchange locations offer currency exchange services nationwide.

Cambodian Riel (KHR): The official unit of exchange for the nation is the Cambodian Riel (KHR). It has the symbol " or "KHR" However, the U.S. Dollar (USD) is widely recognized in many places, especially tourist destinations. Currency exchange services are available in popular tourist locations and large municipalities.

Burmese Kyat (MMK): The Burmese Kyat is the country Myanmar's official currency, and it is represented by the letter "K" or "MMK" Banks, authorized money changers, and airports all provide currency exchange services in major cities.

Before participating in any currency exchange activity, it is advisable to review rates and costs. It's important to be cautious of illegal exchange services on the street that may not supply accurate prices or reliable service since banks and authorized money changers often offer affordable rates.

It's also vital to remember that most major cities and popular tourist destinations in Southeast Asia easily accept major credit cards. To be safe, carrying some local currency with you is always a good idea if you visit smaller shops, markets, or remote spots where card acceptance can be spotty.

Finally, let your bank or credit card company know about your plans to go to Southeast Asia since they could have security measures for international transactions. It will help you prevent any issues or card blockages abroad.

Please be aware that information and conversion rates about currencies may change, so it's always a good idea to double-check with reliable sources or contact local banks for the most up-to-date information.

Accommodation Options

At the Four Seasons Resort Bali in Sayan, Indonesia: This magnificent resort provides breathtaking views, big villas with private pools, and first-rate services. It is nestled away in a gorgeous forest not far from Ubud.

The Datai Langkawi, Malaysia: The Datai Langkawi is a resort in Malaysia that blends luxurious architecture with a pristine natural setting on the gorgeous island of Langkawi. Guests can access a private beach, excellent eating options, and a renowned spa.

Mandarin Oriental, Bangkok, Thailand: On the banks of the Chao Phraya River in Bangkok, Thailand, the iconic Mandarin Oriental hotel blends modern luxury with traditional Thai charm. It includes lavish guest accommodations, renowned dining options, and a tranquil spa.

Amanpulo, Philippines: This exclusive resort offers seclusion and peace. It is situated in the Sulu Sea on a private island. White sand beaches, wealthy homes, and excellent service are everything visitors can enjoy.

Song Saa Private Island, Cambodia: Song Saa Private Island, a private island hideaway in Cambodia, mixes luxury and sustainability. There are lovely overwater villas, a private beach, and several activities, including kayaking and snorkeling.

The Sanchaya, Bintan Island, Indonesia:

Indonesia's Bintan Island, The Sanchaya The exquisite retreat offered by this colonial-style resort is situated on Bintan Island's undeveloped coastline. Visitors may enjoy exploring the island's natural beauty, eating at upscale restaurants, and staying in luxurious villas.

The Nam Hai, Vietnam: The Nam Hai in Vietnam is a beachfront resort with magnificent villas, private pools, an excellent spa, and delicious dining options. It is located along Hoi An's gorgeous coastline.

Banyan Tree Samui, Thailand: The Banyan Tree Samui in Thailand is set on a mountaintop overlooking the Gulf of Thailand and offers breathtaking views and complete solitude from the outer world. There are spa services, delectable cuisine, and spacious villas with private pools accessible to visitors.

Alila Villas Uluwatu, Bali, Indonesia: Bali, Indonesia's Alila Villas Uluwatu, offers stylish villas with private pools and panoramic ocean views. It is situated on a cliff with a picture of the Indian Ocean. It also boasts a spa, an infinity pool, and excellent eating choices.

Six Senses Con Dao, Vietnam: An eco-friendly resort that offers a luxurious and sustainable vacation on the remote Con Dao Islands. Visitors can access private pool homes, empty beaches, and immersion in the natural environment.

64

Chapter Five

Exploring Southeast Asia

Overview of the Countries

Thailand

Exploring Thailand offers fun activities, including cultural riches, stunning scenery, and kind hospitality. Here is a detailed breakdown of what you may expect when exploring Thailand's diverse and intriguing landscapes:

Cultural Heritage: Thailand's extensive cultural past is seen in the country's historical sites, old temples, and customs. Start your journey in Bangkok, where the Grand Palace and Wat Phra Kaew (Temple of the Emerald Buddha) are examples of intricate construction and beautiful architecture. Wat Pho (Temple of the Reclining Buddha) and Wat Arun (Temple of Dawn) are well-known temples. Immerse yourself in the tranquility of these revered temples decorated with golden spires, graceful sculptures, and vibrant murals.

Bustling City Life: Bangkok, the vibrant capital of Thailand, is a busy metropolis brimming with life and diversity. Explore the dynamic street markets, such as Chatuchak Weekend Market, where you can shop for various items, including clothing, handicrafts, and delicious street food. Take a boat excursion along the Chao Phraya River to see the city's combination of old and new, explore the modern shopping malls, and enjoy the vibrant nightlife in areas like Sukhumvit and Silom.

Stunning Beaches and Islands: Thailand is well known for its beautiful islands and tropical beaches. The largest island, Phuket, offers a mix of lively nightlife, water sports, and serene beaches, including Patong, Kata, and Karon. The Phi Phi Islands, shown in "The Beach," contain stunning limestone cliffs and waters ideal for diving and snorkeling. Other well-known locations include the peaceful island of Koh Lanta, the towering karsts of Krabi, and Koh Samui's palm-fringed beaches.

Natural Wonders: Thailand's natural beauty will leave nature lovers speechless. Explore Khao Yai National Park's lush woods and cascading waterfalls, or explore the northern to find the mist-shrouded highlands of Chiang Mai and Chiang Rai. Learn about the Elephant Nature Park, where you may interact ethically and responsibly with rescued elephants. Explore the breathtaking scenery of Pai or the natural magnificence of Khao Sok National Park for an excursion off the beaten road.

Floating Markets & Food Delights:

1. Visit floating markets like Damnoen Saduak and Amphawa to experience Thailand's burgeoning food industry.
2. Navigate the canals while enjoying the local way of life as vendors sell fresh produce, delectable street food, and traditional handicrafts from their boats.
3. Taste the many flavors of Thai cuisine, from hot curries and tangy salads to

flavorful noodles and delectable desserts.
4. Learn the secrets of Thai cooking and bring the flavors of Thailand home with you by enrolling in a cooking class.

Festivals and Traditions: Thailand has a plethora of vibrant festivals throughout the year that provide a rich cultural experience. Celebrate Songkran, the Thai New Year, in April when locals and visitors engage in a joyful water fight to symbolize washing away the previous year's troubles. Behold the fascinating Loy Krathong celebration, celebrated on the full moon of the 12th lunar month when people release wonderfully decorated floats across rivers, lakes, and canals. Fireworks and traditional entertainment follow the festival.

It's important to follow local customs and traditions while visiting Thailand, such as dressing when visiting temples and exhibiting respect at sacred places. Interacting with the locals can help you better understand the nation's culture and create enduring memories of your journey through this intriguing region. Since Thailand offers many opportunities for each visitor, remember to plan your trip around your interests and desired experiences. Thailand promises to be an incredible and fulfilling experience, regardless of whether you're looking for adventure, relaxation, cultural immersion, or a combination of all of these.

Map of Indonesia

Indonesia

Southeast Asian country Indonesia is a beautiful place known for its extensive natural wonders, stunning scenery, and rich cultural heritage. It is the largest archipelago in the world, with over 17,000 islands, and offers travelers looking for adventure, pleasure, and cultural immersion in various activities. This comprehensive book will examine many aspects of experiencing Indonesia, including its geography, culture, well-known tourist destinations, and useful travel advice.

Geography: Geographically, Indonesia connects the continents of Asia and Australia by being situated between the Indian Ocean and the Pacific Ocean. Its maritime boundaries reach Singapore, the Philippines, and Australia, and it shares borders with Papua New Guinea, Timor-Leste, and Malaysia. The varied terrain of the nation includes imposing volcanoes, dense forests, stunning beaches, and bright coral reefs. Sumatra, Java, Bali,

Kalimantan (Borneo), Sulawesi, and Papua are among Indonesia's main islands.

Culture: Due to its history of colonization and trade, Indonesia is a melting pot of many cultural influences. Numerous ethnic groups, including Javanese, Sundanese, Batak, Balinese, and many others, comprise the nation's population. The traditions, languages, music, dances, and cuisines of each tribe are unique. Although Christianity, Hinduism, Buddhism, and indigenous traditions are all followed, Islam is the dominant religion in the country.

Popular Destinations:

Bali: Also referred to as the "Island of the Gods," Bali is a well-liked tourist destination because of its breathtaking beauty, vibrant arts scene, and spiritual retreats. Visitors may explore historic temples like Uluwatu and Tanah Lot, participate in water sports in Nusa Dua, or unwind on Seminyak and Kuta's world-class beaches.

Jakarta: Jakarta, Indonesia's capital city, offers a mix of traditional and modern attractions. Visit the National Museum and the Old Town (Kota Tua) to learn about the region's rich history and culture, the vibrant Tanah Abang markets, modern malls, and nightlife districts to indulge in shopping and entertainment.

Yogyakarta: The UNESCO-listed Borobudur and Prambanan temples in Yogyakarta, a cultural hub on the island of Java, are renowned for their traditional Javanese architecture and Buddhist and Hindu influences. In addition, Yogyakarta is famous for its magnificent Kraton (Sultan's Palace), puppet shows, and traditional batik clothing.

Komodo National Park: The Komodo dragons, the largest reptiles in the world, may be found at Komodo National Park, which lies in eastern Indonesia. Visitors may go on boat cruises to get up close and personal with these fascinating creatures. They can also go snorkeling and diving in the park's pristine marine ecosystem.

Raja Ampat: Raja Ampat is a tropical haven in West Papua renowned for its incredible marine life. In its clean waters, snorkelers and divers may explore vibrant coral reefs, get to know unusual fish species, and take in the stunning underwater environment.

Practical Travel Tips: Check your country's visa requirements before traveling to Indonesia. While some countries may need to apply for visas in advance, others may be able to get them upon arrival or benefit from visa-free entry policies.

Weather: The tropical climate of Indonesia varies by location and island. Consider the current weather patterns and make your travel arrangements accordingly. Be prepared for high humidity, especially along the shore, and plan for rainy seasons in certain areas.

Transportation: In Indonesia, there are many different ways to go around. These include domestic airplanes, trains, buses, and ferries. Large cities have public transportation, however.

Map of Vietnam

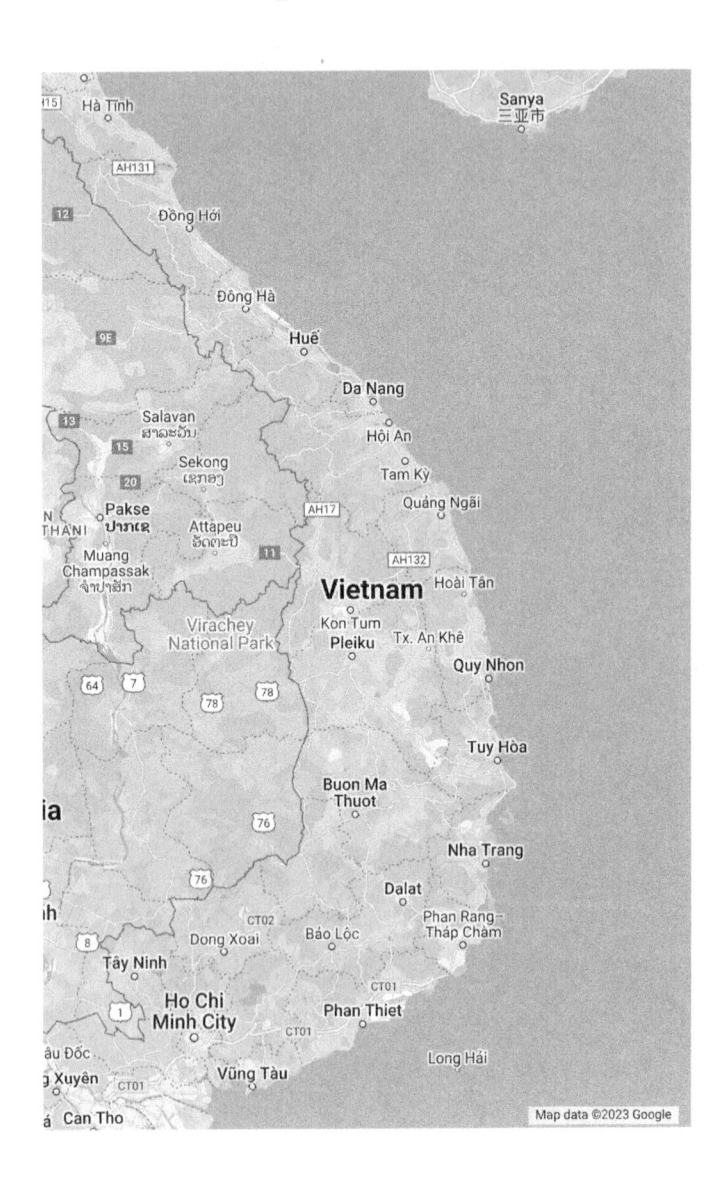

Vietnam

Vietnam is a fascinating country in Southeast Asia with a vibrant culture, amazing natural beauty, and a long history. Vietnam offers visitors many experiences, from bustling cities to serene rural landscapes. This comprehensive book covers various topics about visiting Vietnam, including its geography, culture, famous landmarks, and useful travel advice.

Geography: On the eastern coast of the Indochinese Peninsula, Vietnam is bounded by China to the north, Laos, Cambodia to the west, and the South China Sea to the east and south. The country's diverse landscape has stunning coastal regions, lush mountains, dense forests, and productive river deltas. The three main regions of Vietnam are Northern Vietnam, Central Vietnam, and Southern Vietnam.

Culture: Vietnam's history and wide range of ethnic groups have significantly impacted the country's rich cultural heritage. Most people are Vietnamese, although there are sizable minorities of Tay, Thai, Muong, and Hmong. Although several regional dialects and minority languages are widely used, Vietnamese is the official language. Folk ballads and the distinctive Vietnamese water puppets exemplify the country's well-known traditional music. The savory dishes in Vietnamese cuisine, such as pho (noodle soup) and banh mi (baguette sandwiches), are famous worldwide.

Popular Destinations:

Hanoi: The capital of Vietnam, Hanoi, mixes traditional beauty with modern vitality. Discover the narrow streets, ancient sites like the Ho Chi Minh Mausoleum and the Temple of Literature, and the vibrant street food scene of the Old Quarter.

Halong Bay: The stunning limestone karsts from the bay's emerald waters have been recognized as a UNESCO World Heritage site. Explore the tunnels and floating settlements while enjoying a boat ride around the bay and the mesmerizing sunset views.

Hoi An: A quaint medieval village in Central Vietnam, is a UNESCO World Heritage site. While admiring the well-preserved architecture and meandering through lantern-lit alleys, explore the vibrant local markets. Additionally, Hoi An is renowned for its tailors, where you may get specially created clothing for you.

Ho Chi Minh City: Often known as Saigon, is a bustling metropolis in southern Vietnam that offers a vibrant urban experience. Discover historical sites like the Reunification Palace and the War Remnants Museum, indulge in delectable street food, and enjoy lively nightlife.

Sapa: Situated in the nation's north, Sapa is well-known for its breathtaking rice terraces and trekking opportunities. Explore the ethnic minority communities nearby, take in the beauty of the mountains, and discover the area's unique culture.

Practical Travel Tips:

Visa: Check your country's visa requirements before traveling to Vietnam. Depending on your nationality, you may need to apply for a ticket in advance or get one upon arrival.

Weather: Vietnam's climate differs depending on where you are. The country has two rainy and dry seasons in a tropical monsoon environment. Planning your journey around the local weather patterns is the best action.

Transportation: Domestic planes, trains, buses, and taxis are all part of Vietnam's well-developed transportation network. In cities, motorcycles are a widespread mode of transportation; nonetheless, whether riding or crossing the street, use caution.

Currency: The national currency is the Vietnamese Dong (VND). Since credit and debit cards are usually accepted in big cities and tourist areas, carrying cash and cards is advised.

Cultural Etiquette: Respect the regional traditions and practices while visiting temples and other religious sites. Dress sartorially.

Map of Malaysia

Malaysia

Malaysia is a fascinating country in Southeast Asia, known for its vibrant cities, stunning landscape, and mouthwatering cuisine. Visitors may choose from a wide range of experiences in Malaysia, from bustling cities to serene natural wonders. This comprehensive guide covers a wide range of Malaysia-related topics, including its geography, culture, famous landmarks, and useful travel advice.

Geography: Malaysia, which borders Thailand and has maritime borders with Indonesia and Vietnam, is situated on the Malay Peninsula in continental Southeast Asia. It also includes the states of Sabah and Sarawak on the island of Borneo. Luxuriant rainforests, towering mountains, attractive beaches, and diverse flora characterize the nation's landscape. Malaysia's three main areas are Peninsular Malaysia, East Malaysia (Borneo), and the Federal Territories of Kuala Lumpur and Putrajaya.

Culture: Malaysia is a melting pot of cultures with influences from indigenous, Chinese, Malay, and Indian customs. Malays, Chinese, Indians, and many indigenous tribes make up the population, and they all contribute to the intricate cultural fabric of the nation. Although English is widely used, Bahasa Malaysia (Malay) is the official language. Malaysia is well known for its vibrant celebrations, including Deepavali, Chinese New Year, and Hari Raya Aidilfitri (Eid al-Fitr), allowing visitors to participate in various cultural events.

Popular Destinations:

Kuala Lumpur: The capital of Malaysia, Kuala Lumpur, is a vibrant city home to various contemporary buildings, iconic monuments, and lively street markets. Visit the stunning Petronas Twin Towers, the thriving Chinatown and Little India areas, and indulge in the Jalan Alor's gastronomic treats.

Penang: Also known as the "Pearl of the Orient," this vibrant island resort combines colonial grandeur, a rich past, and mouthwatering street food. Learn about George Town, a UNESCO World Heritage Site, see places like Khoo Kongsi and Fort Cornwallis, and sample the legendary Penang Assam Laksa.

Langkawi: The Langkawi archipelago of lovely islands off the west coast of Malaysia provides pristine beaches, lush woods, and a laid-back island lifestyle. Discover magnificent beaches like Pantai Cenang, travel to Mount Cincang via cable car, and shop at duty-free stores.

Borneo: On the island of Borneo, the Malaysian states of Sabah and Sarawak offer incredible natural beauty. Rich rainforests, unusual fauna, and Mount Kinabalu are all found in these locations. Take a Kinabatangan River tour to witness animals, see the Sepilok Orangutan Rehabilitation Center, and hike in Mulu National Park.

Malacca: A UNESCO World Heritage site, has elements of Portuguese, Dutch, and British architecture and culture. Take a river boat to see the city's magnificence, explore ancient places like St. Paul's Church and A Famosa Fort, and wander down Jonker Street to locate specialized stores and cuisine.

Practical Travel Tips:

Visa: Ensure you are familiar with the visa requirements for your country of residency before flying to Malaysia. Some nations may need access to enter, while others may be given one upon arrival or permitted admission without a visa for a predetermined time.

Weather: Malaysia has high humidity levels year-round due to its tropical climate. Be careful of the monsoon seasons and the potentially hot and humid weather they bring while preparing for your vacation, as their impact might vary depending on where you travel.

Transportation: The modern transportation network in Malaysia consists of domestic airplanes, trains, buses, and taxis. Public transit is often available in large cities, and popular ride-hailing services like Grab are readily available. Renting a vehicle is another option for going to farther-flung destinations.

Currency: The Malaysian Ringgit (MYR) is the country of Malaysia's official currency. ATMs are commonly accessible, and credit cards are often accepted. Cash is essential to have on hand for small shops and neighborhood markets.

Health and Safety: Make sure your travel insurance covers medical expenses for your well-being and security. In certain places, it is recommended to consume bottled water, maintain strict cleanliness standards, and take the required safety steps to avoid illnesses caused by mosquitoes. Respect local regulations and be aware of your surroundings for your safety.

Etiquette: As a cosmopolitan nation, Malaysia has many ethnic and social norms. Following regional traditions is crucial, such as removing your shoes before entering a house or a place of worship and wearing modestly, there are necessary. Additionally, greetings include a handshake, and items are presented and accepted with the right hand.

Food: Malay, Chinese, and Indian cuisines all affect Malaysia's great range of flavors. Don't miss the chance to try local delicacies like nasi lemak (coconut rice), roti canai (Indian flatbread), satay (grilled skewers), and laksa (hot noodle soup).

Exploring Malaysia is a thrilling experience because of the country's unique blend of cultural variety, magnificent natural beauty, and friendly people. By paying heed to some helpful recommendations, you may make the most of your vacation and leave this beautiful, fascinating nation with treasured memories.

Map of Philippines

Philippines

Southeast Asia's Philippines is an archipelago of more than 7,000 islands. Visitors may engage in a variety of activities around the nation. It is renowned for its magnificent beaches, diverse marine life, extensive cultural history, and kind friendliness. In this thorough guide, we'll cover many topics related to traveling to the Philippines, including its geography, culture, well-known tourist attractions, and practical travel tips.

Geography: Geographically speaking, the Philippines is located in the western Pacific Ocean and has maritime boundaries to the north and south with both Taiwan and Indonesia. Mindanao in the south, Visayas in the center, and Luzon in the north comprise the nation's three primary geographic regions. Pure beaches, warm jungles, volcanoes, rice terraces, and unusual geological formations are just a few of the Philippines' stunning natural attractions.

Culture: A blend of indigenous customs, Malay cultural components, and Spanish and American colonial influences make up Filipino culture. Malay people comprise the bulk of the population, although there is also a significant Chinese, Spanish, and American influence. The people of the Philippines are renowned for being kind, enjoying music and dance, and having exuberant festivals. Christianity, especially Roman Catholicism, is the most widely practiced religion in the nation.

Popular Destinations:
The island country of Palawan, sometimes known as the "Last Frontier," is famed for its stunning vistas and clear seas. Visit the lovely underground river in Puerto Princesa, one of the many islands in El Nido, or the colorful coral reefs at the Tubbataha Reefs Natural Park.
Boracay: is a well-known island paradise with pristine white sand beaches and vibrant nightlife. While relaxing on the magnificent

beaches and engaging in water activities like kiteboarding and snorkeling, savor delectable seafood and regional cuisine.

Cebu: The booming tourist attraction of Cebu is home to various artificial and natural treasures. Visit Cebu City's historical sights, Badian's magnificent Kawasan Falls, and Oslob to go whale shark swimming.

Bohol has unique natural features, including the famed Chocolate Hills and Tarsier reserves. Take in the breathtaking surroundings, see the centuries-old Baclayon Church, and float along the Loboc River while enjoying a classic Filipino meal.

Siargao: Known as the top surfing location in the Philippines, Siargao Island draws visitors from all over the globe. Explore the magnificent beaches and lagoons, soak in the laid-back island vibe, and surf the well-known Cloud 9 waves.

Practical Travel Tips:

Visa: Ensure you are familiar with the visa requirements for your country of residency before flying to the Philippines. Some nationalities may be eligible for visa-on-arrival or visa-free travel for a limited period.

Weather: In the Philippines, the wet season is from May to October, and the dry season is from November to April. Typhoon seasons should be considered as you travel, particularly from July to October.

Transportation: Domestic flights are the most feasible way to travel between islands. Additionally, ferries and boats connect several locations. Buses, tricycles, and jeepneys are some of the available local transportation alternatives. In urban areas, ride-hailing services like Grab are available.

Currency: The Philippine Peso (PHP) is the nation of the Philippines' official currency. Major credit cards are accepted in tourist regions, and ATMs are readily available. Small enterprises and local markets depend on having cash on hand.

Health and Safety: Ensure your travel insurance covers medical costs for your well-being and security. Follow basic safety rules, such as being cautious with your possessions and avoiding vacant areas at night. To prevent contracting a mosquito-borne illness, remember to stay hydrated, use insect repellent, wear protective clothing, and take other crucial precautions.

Etiquette: Filipino people's generous welcome and respect are well known. It is usual to greet people with a grin and a handshake. When visiting places of worship, dress modestly and respect local customs.

Cuisine: Filipino food is a delectable blend of ingredients influenced by cooking methods from the Malay, Chinese, and Spanish empires. Don't miss the chance to try meals like lechon (roasted pig), sinigang (sour soup), and adobo (marinated beef), which are famous across the world. Street food is a popular and excellent alternative to take into consideration.

Being absorbed in the local culture and seeing the stunning natural scenery are just two of the many exciting experiences that come with exploring the Philippines. By following this helpful advice, you can make the most of your trip and create priceless memories in this stunning country.

Map of Singapore

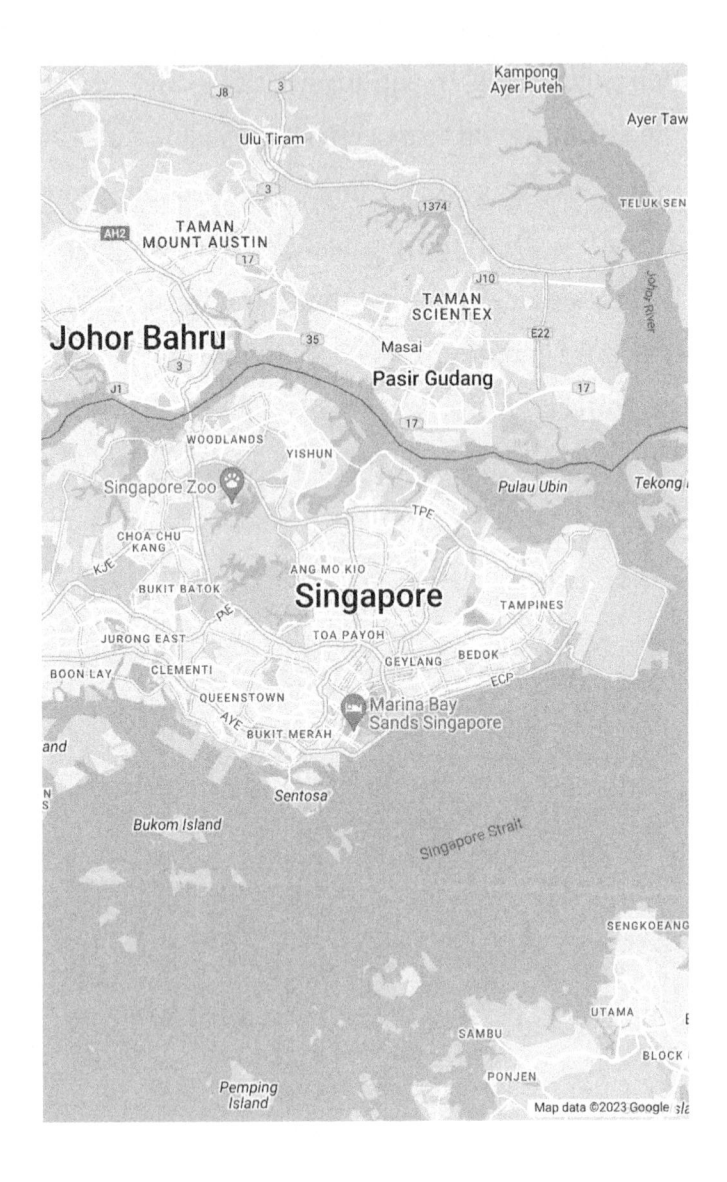

Singapore

A city-state in Southeast Asia, Singapore is recognized for its cutting-edge construction, array of cultural influences, and efficient infrastructure. Despite its tiny size, Singapore offers a variety of experiences, including contemporary architecture, lush green parks, and vibrant street markets. The geography, culture, important sites, and practical travel advice of Singapore will all be covered in detail in this comprehensive travel book.

Geography: Singapore is located near the southernmost point of the Malay Peninsula, just off the coast of Malaysia. The island city-state is connected to the continent by two causeways. Singapore is a significant hub for international trade and the blending of cultures due to its convenient location. Despite being small, Singapore offers a stunning skyline, thoughtfully managed urban growth, and a variety of green spaces.

Culture: Singapore is a multicultural culture that seamlessly blends influences from diverse ethnic groups and celebrates variety. Chinese, Malay, Indian, and Eurasian are Singapore's four primary ethnic groups, and each has a unique cultural contribution to give. English, Malay, Mandarin, and Tamil are the country's official languages, highlighting its linguistic diversity. Its festivals, traditional arts, and mouthwatering cuisine display Singapore's cultural legacy.

Popular Attractions:

Marina Bay Sands: The renowned integrated resort complex known as Marina Bay Sands is a must-see sight in Singapore. Explore the upmarket shopping sector and take in the striking architectural architecture and magnificent views from the SkyPark Observation Deck. Don't miss the mesmerizing Spectra, light, and water show at Marina Bay Sands.

Gardens by the Bay: this is a must-see sight in the middle of the city. Visit the amazing

Supertree Grove, the renowned Cloud Forest, and the Flower Dome Conservatories as you stroll along the picturesque waterfront promenade.

Sentosa Island: Tanjong Beach, Adventure Cove Waterpark, S.E.A. Aquarium, and Universal Studios Singapore are just a few attractions on Sentosa Island, a popular tourist destination. Enjoy exhilarating rides, discover marine life, and relax on stunning beaches.

Chinatown: To properly appreciate Singapore's Chinese heritage, visit Chinatown. Explore bustling street markets, breathtaking temples like the Buddha Tooth Relic Temple, and indulge in local Chinese cuisine.

Little India: Discover the gorgeous hues, alluring fragrances, and rich Indian culture in Little India. Discover the Sri Veeramakaliamman Temple, peruse the neighborhood shops, and indulge in real Indian food.

Practical Travel Tips:

Visa: Ensure you know the relevant tickets for your country of residency before traveling to Singapore. Entry without a key is permitted temporarily for many nations. Verify that your passport has at least a six-month remaining validity.

Weather: Singapore experiences year-round excessive humidity in a tropical climate. Wear breathable, light clothing and be prepared for frequent showers. Carrying an umbrella or raincoat is advised.

Transportation: Singapore boasts a reliable MRT (Mass Rapid Transit) system and buses and taxis. Use the EZ-Link card to pay for transit fares swiftly. Walking is an extra option because the city-state is so compact.

Currency: Singapore's official currency is the Singapore Dollar (SGD). Most businesses usually accept credit cards, and ATMs are widely available.

Etiquette: Due to Singapore's stringent laws and regulations, it is crucial to follow local customs. There are fines linked with jaywalking and littering, and chewing gum is not permitted. Before entering a home and various places of worship, it is traditional to take off your shoes.

Food: Singapore is a culinary wonderland with many regional and international cuisines. It would help if you didn't miss out on specialties like Hainanese chicken rice, chili crab, laksa, and roti prata. An excellent place to find delicious local food at a fair price is at hawker centers.

Explore Singapore to find a mix of modernism, ethnic diversity, and natural beauty. Using these helpful ideas, you may make the most of your trip and experience everything this dynamic city-state offers.

Map of Cambodia

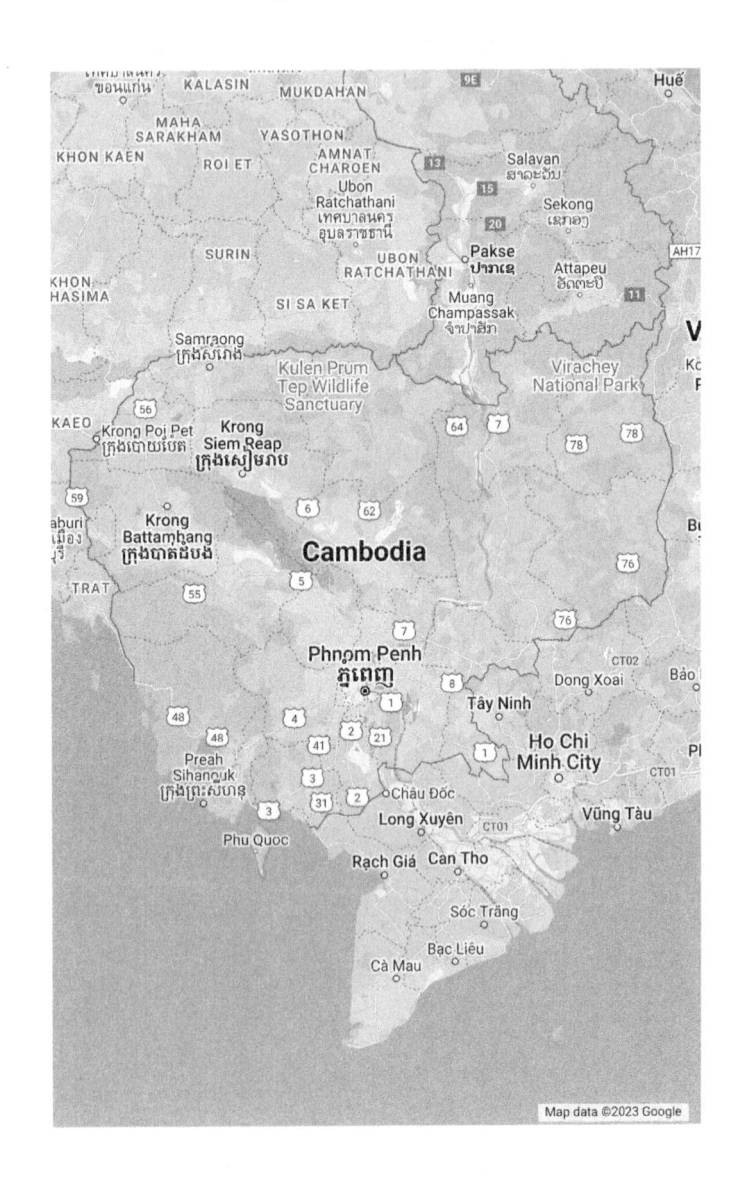

Cambodia

Cambodia is located in Southeast Asia and has incredible natural beauty, history, and culture. From majestic beaches and lush forests to ancient temples and bustling towns, Cambodia offers various travel experiences. This book will cover the many facets of traveling to Cambodia, giving you accurate and comprehensive information to help you get the most out of your trip.

Historical Significance: The ancient Khmer Empire, which dominated a large portion of Southeast Asia from the ninth to the fifteenth century, is inextricably linked to the history of Cambodia. Angkor Wat, one of the largest religious structures in the world and a UNESCO World Heritage site, is the most obvious representation of this empire. Travelers may see the magnificence of temples like Bayon, Ta Prohm, and Banteay Srei, embellished with stunning sculptures and steeped in spiritual importance while exploring the ancient city of Angkor.

Vibrant Cities: The capital of Cambodia, Phnom Penh, is a vibrant city that skillfully blends traditional Khmer architecture with contemporary development. To fully appreciate Cambodia's rich cultural heritage, visit the Royal Palace, Silver Pagoda, and National Museum. The town of Siem Reap, which serves as the entrance to Angkor Wat, offers a unique blend of local markets, a vibrant nightlife, and a variety of food options.

Cultural Experiences: Theravada Buddhism is firmly ingrained in Cambodian culture, and there are many possibilities to investigate this side of Buddhism. You may go to serene monasteries, take part in meditation retreats, or attend a customary Buddhist ceremony. The nation also hosts vibrant festivals like the Water Festival and the Khmer New Year, which provide a glimpse into regional cultures and traditions.

Natural Wonders: Besides its historical and cultural sites, Cambodia also offers breathtaking natural scenery. Visitors may get a sample of traditional Cambodian life in the area, dotted with rice fields, little communities, and stunning landscapes. Tonle Sap Lake, the biggest freshwater lake in Southeast Asia, is a UNESCO Biosphere Reserve featuring floating communities, various bird species, and unusual ecosystems. Coastal regions like Sihanoukville and Koh Rong provide stunning beaches, beautiful seas, and chances for snorkeling, diving, and leisure.

Responsible Tourism: When traveling to Cambodia, practicing responsible tourism is important. Support regional companies and communities, observe cultural norms, and engage in ethical tourism while being environmentally conscious. Numerous honest tour operators provide engaging experiences that help the neighborhood.

Practical Considerations: When organizing a vacation to Cambodia, consider the weather.

The dry season, which lasts from November to April, is the ideal time to visit because of the milder temperatures and less rain. Conversely, the wet season, which lasts from May to October, may provide special experiences like seeing stunning scenery and running into fewer visitors. Before you go, confirm that you have all the required vaccinations, travel insurance, and visas.

Finally, traveling to Cambodia is a great experience due to its fascinating history, vibrant cities, cultural interactions, stunning natural surroundings, and measures to promote responsible tourism. Cambodia has plenty to offer everyone, whether they are drawn to historic temples, interested in local customs, or seeking leisure on stunning beaches. If you spend time there, you'll acquire enduring memories of this interesting nation and a deeper comprehension of its fascinating past.

Map of Laos

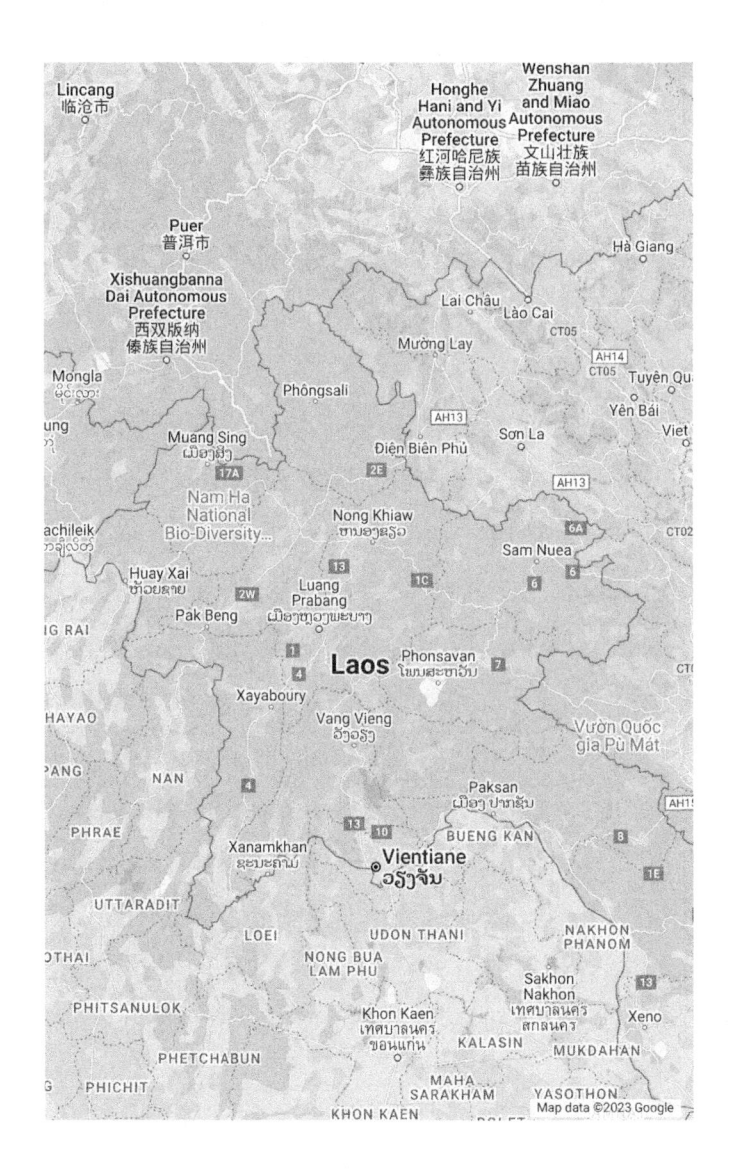

Laos

Laos, sometimes referred to as the "Land of a Million Elephants," is a treasure of Southeast Asia that combines tranquility, rich culture, and scenic beauty. This thorough guide provides accurate and complete information about traveling in Laos to maximize your time there.

Cultural Heritage: Laos's numerous temples, monasteries, and religious festivals attest to the country's strong Theravada Buddhist heritage. The UNESCO World Heritage site Luang Prabang serves as the country of Laos's cultural center. Its historic temples, including Wat Xieng Thong and Wat Mai, stand out for their elaborate architecture and exquisite adornment. A cherished custom not to be missed is the daily alms-giving ritual, where monks gather money from residents and tourists.

Natural Wonders:

Beautiful natural scenery across Laos, including verdant woods, tranquil waterfalls, and flowing rivers. The Mekong River, the country's lifeblood, offers breathtaking boat tours, river cruises, and opportunities to interact with people who live along the riverside. Kayaking, caving, and trekking are just a few outdoor pursuits in Vang Vieng, a quaint town tucked away among gorgeous karst mountains. With its serene riverine setting and uncommon Irrawaddy dolphins, the 4,000 Islands (Si Phan Don) locale in southern Laos offers a calming refuge.

Authentic Experiences: There are several unique and genuine activities available in Laos. You may learn about traditional ways of life by visiting nearby villages, participating in handicraft activities, or even staying with a local family. Travelers are fascinated by the secrets of the past as they explore the Plain of Jars, an archaeological site in central Laos.

Outdoor Adventures: Adventures in the great outdoors: Laos has much to offer travelers. The northern area, especially around Luang Namtha and Muang Ngoi, is accessible for steep terrain trekking, contacts with ethnic minorities, and stays in eco-lodges. The coffee plantations, waterfalls, and picturesque drives in the Bolaven Plateau in southern Laos are well-known. Kayaking is possible on the Nam Ou River, which also offers views of northern Laos' wild splendor.

Slow and Serene Pace: Laos is known for its more relaxed way of life, which contrasts nicely with the hectic pace of cities. Visitors may unwind, rest, and take in the area's natural beauty in a peaceful environment. Enjoy a stroll through the narrow streets of Luang Prabang, a cup of freshly made coffee at a riverside café, or just a sunset view of the Mekong River.

Practical Considerations: When planning travel to Laos, consider weather trends. The dry season, which lasts from November to

April, is the ideal time to visit because of the milder temperatures and less rain. The lush and bright landscapes have their attractiveness during the rainy season, which lasts from May to October. Before you go, confirm that you have all the required vaccinations, travel insurance, and visas.

Finally, Laos's rich cultural legacy, stunning scenery, and tranquil environment make for a superb vacation experience. Laos captivates the hearts of tourists looking for a genuine and peaceful experience with its breathtaking temples, quaint villages, and natural beauty. Your connection to this extraordinary place will grow due to your immersion in the nation's rich traditions and appreciation of its natural beauty.

Map of Burma

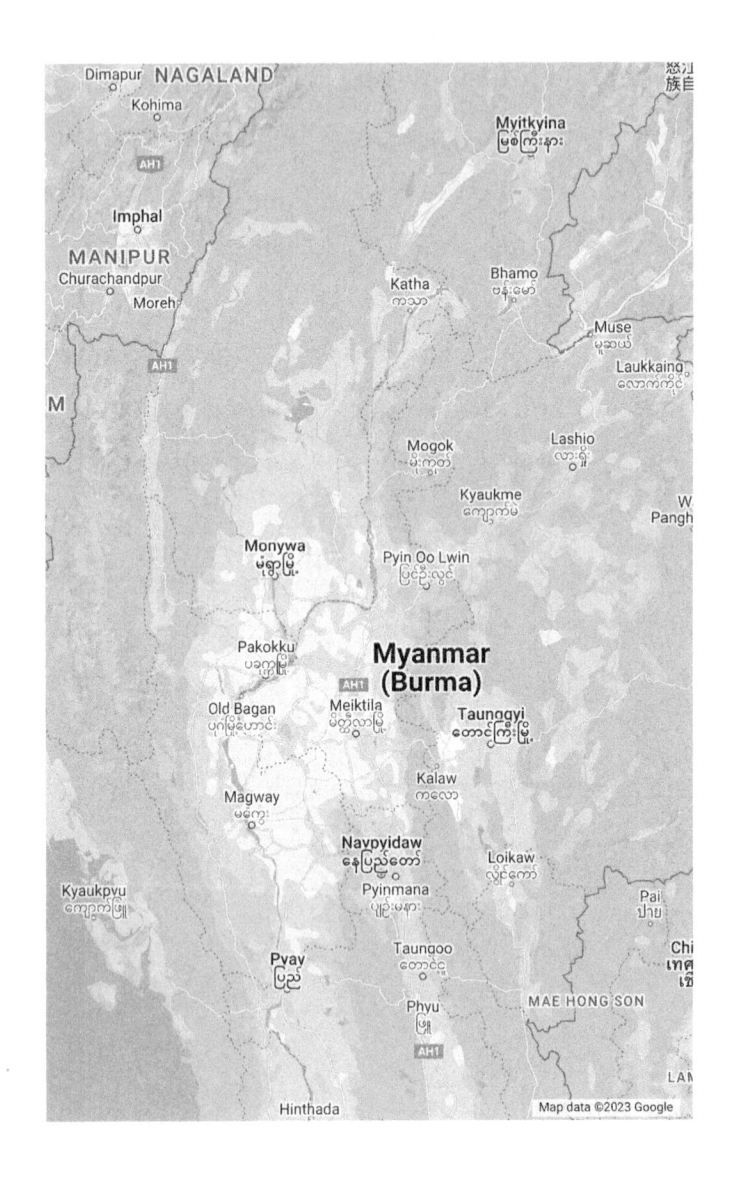

Burma

Formerly known as Burma, Myanmar is a fascinating country in Southeast Asia that offers a wealth of cultural treasures, breathtaking landscapes, and a distinctive blend of cultures. This specific book makes an effort to provide accurate and comprehensive information on traveling in Myanmar, assisting you in making the most of your trip to this fantastic area.

Historical and Cultural Gems: Myanmar has a long history and a well-ingrained Buddhist culture that permeates all aspects of daily life. The Shwedagon Pagoda, a gilded masterpiece and one of the most important sites in Buddhism, can be found in Yangon, the country's former capital. The cultural center of Mandalay is known for its regal palaces, ancient temples, and bustling markets. Over 2,000 beautifully preserved temples and pagodas may be found at Bagan, an archaeological wonder that gives a window into the nation's storied past.

Beautiful scenery: Myanmar has a wide variety of beautiful scenery. You may see the peculiar floating gardens, stilted huts, and traditional fishing methods of the local Intha people at Inle Lake, tucked between undulating hills in Shan State. The Golden Rock (Kyaiktiyo Pagoda), which is precariously perched on the side of a cliff, offers a breathtaking panoramic view of the region. Hsipaw and Kalaw are the entry points to magnificent walking routes that take you through picturesque settings and into contact with ethnic minority people.

Myanmar offers a variety of opportunities to immerse oneself in its diverse cultures and exceptional experiences. Visit local markets to see the vibrant tapestry of daily life, go to far-off regions to meet the locals, or take part in a meditation retreat to learn more about Myanmar's spiritual side. Puppetry, traditional dance, and vibrant celebrations like Thingyan

(Water Festival) provide glimpses into the nation's cultural heritage.

Beautiful beaches and unspoiled islands may be found along Myanmar's coastline in the Bay of Bengal and the Andaman Sea. Ngapali Beach offers a tranquil and perfect relaxing setting with its palm-lined shoreline and sparkling waters. Divers will find the Mergui Archipelago, a group of over 800 islands, a hidden gem because of its pristine coral reefs, abundant marine life, and solitary island getaways.

Responsible Tourism: It is essential to practice accountable tourism while visiting Myanmar. Respect the local traditions, customs, and places of worship. Practice sustainable tourism by patronizing regional businesses, reducing your environmental impact, and showing respect for the neighborhood. Be mindful of cultural sensitivity, especially while interacting with people from ethnic minorities.

Practical Advice: Before traveling to Myanmar, make sure you have the necessary visas, shots, and travel insurance in place. They are learning about the weather patterns since the country experiences a monsoon season from May to October. Most people think the best time to travel is from November through February because of the warmer weather.

In conclusion, visiting Myanmar offers a chance to go on a journey of discovery thanks to its historical landmarks, stunning vistas, and extensive cultural heritage. Visitors looking for a true and immersive experience are enthralled by Myanmar's glittering pagodas, vibrant markets, serene lakes, and immaculate beaches. You will have priceless experiences and a deeper understanding of this intriguing area by embracing the local traditions, interacting with the populace, and admiring its natural beauty.

Off the Beaten Path Destinations

Southeast Asia is a vast and diverse region with many undiscovered gems waiting to be discovered. Here are a few locations to think about if you're looking for an off-the-beaten-path holiday experience:

Umphang, Thailand: The Umphang National Park, which is home to a variety of species, including elephants, tigers, and bears, is located in the remote mountain hamlet of Umphang in Thailand. This area also boasts some of the country's most breathtaking scenery.

Kratie, Cambodia: Irrawaddy dolphins may be seen swimming in the Mekong River at Kratie, Cambodia, a small community that is well-known for them. Kratie is a great place to study Khmer history and culture.

Quy Nhon, Vietnam: Vietnam's Quy Nhon is a coastal city famous for its fine seafood, wonderful beaches, and breathtaking views of the South China Sea. Seeing the nearby Cham ruins from Quy Nhon is a great idea.

Champasak, Laos: This region of Laos is home to several Khmer structures, most notably the remains of Wat Phu, one of the most important Southeast Asian archaeological sites. Champasak is a great place for trekking and getting to know the locals.

Hsipaw, Myanmar: This little village in Myanmar is well-known for its stunning scenery and relaxed atmosphere. Hsipaw is a great place for trekking, exploring the local neighborhoods, and learning about Shan culture.

These are only a few of Southeast Asia's many off-the-beaten-path locations. With so much to see and do, you will find the perfect place to escape the crowds and experience something distinctive.

You may also wish to take into account the following other Southeast Asian off-the-beaten-path destinations:

- **Luang Namtha, Laos:** With mountains and forests around it, this remote community in the country's north is a great place to go cycling, trekking, and bird-watching.
- **Don Det Island, Laos:** Don Det Island in Laos is a charming location to unwind on the beach, explore the nearby villages, and go kayaking.
- **Koh Rong Island, Cambodia:** This beautiful island off the coast of Cambodia is renowned for its pristine waters, white sand beaches, and relaxed atmosphere.
- **Kapas Island, Malaysia:** which is a small island off the country's coast, is well known for its lush forests, crystal-clear waters, and stunning beaches.

- **Taman Negara National Park, Malaysia:** Elephants, tigers, and rhinoceroses may all be found in Malaysia's Taman Negara National Park, along with many more animals. It's a great place for camping, hiking, and exploring.

Whatever your hobbies, Southeast Asia probably has a destination off the beaten path that's perfect for you. So deviate from the path of least resistance and explore this amazing region's hidden treasures!

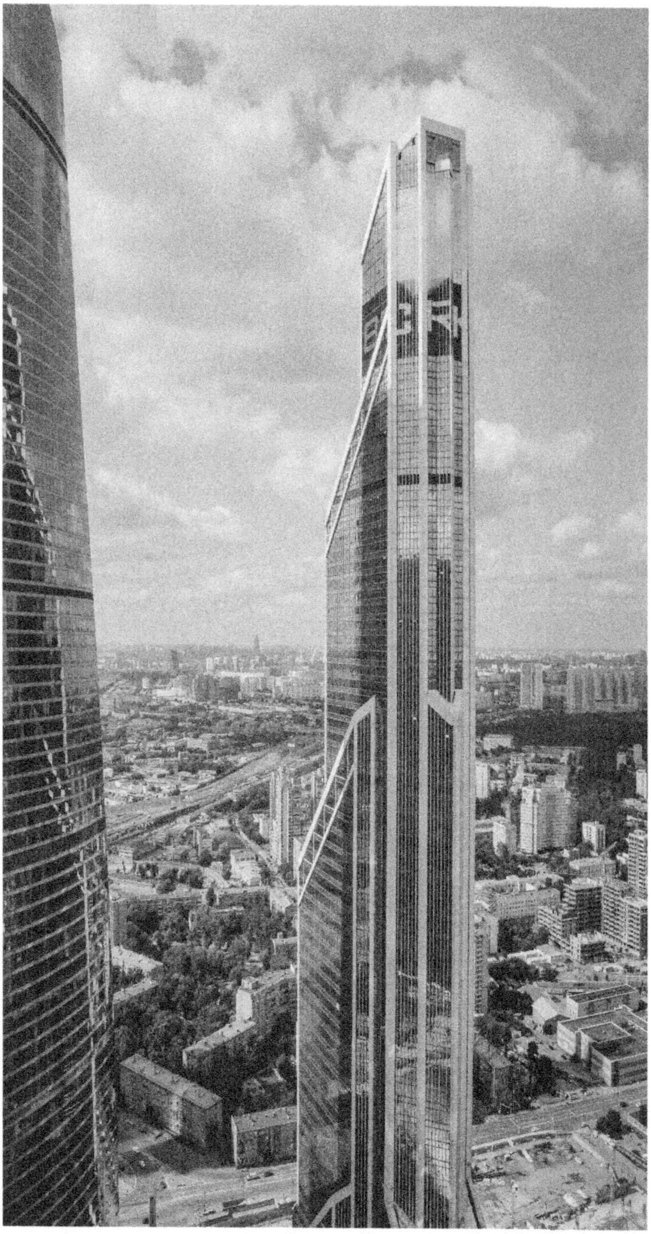

Chapter Six

Food and cuisine

The cuisine of Southeast Asia is among the best in the world. While every country offers a variety of delicious treats, in our opinion, Thailand and Vietnam—with Malaysia coming in a close second—are the standouts in the region.

Although what constitutes superb food varies greatly from person to person—for instance, we seem to be in the minority in Burma's rich, thick curries—it is quite rare to have a bad meal in Vietnam or Thailand.

In light of the fact that there are regional and even local variations on staple foods, it would be incorrect to think of cuisines as existing in distinct, exclusively national blocks. With a few highlights, the aforementioned demonstrates some rather broad strokes. Only the beginning is ahead!

Burma:

Burma Yangon, the country's economic hub, is the perfect location to sample a wide variety of regional delicacies, while Mandalay, in the country's north, also offers many options. In many ways, Burma's diverse cuisine explains the migration from India and Bangladesh to Thailand, much like in terms of culture. Think fresh noodles, iced coffee and beverages, and rich, thick, oily curries.

Mohinga, possibly the country's dish, is a must-try food. The base is made up of rice noodles and fish paste, which are often paired with garlic, onions, and lemongrass. Optional toppings include banana tree roots, chickpeas, or fishcake, although many variations exist.

Cambodia: Siem Reap is the center of Cambodian food culture, which isn't necessarily Khmer-centric. The cuisine of Cambodia is the most understated in Southeast Asia. Alongside grilled steak, chicken, and fish are soups and curries that include fish. Many dishes start with pungent prahok or fermented fish sauce, and the underlying spice is often milder in flavor than in Thailand.

During the genocide of the 1970s and the ensuing years of instability, much information about Cambodian food was lost, yet many people have tried to recall memories of traditional meals precisely.

Amok is a must-try meal. Freshwater fish fillets are wrapped in banana leaves and covered with a coconut custard made of eggs, fish sauce, palm sugar, and a curry seasoning blend that includes lemongrass, turmeric, Using heat to produce a scuffle-like texture, galangal, kaffir lime zest, garlic, shallots, and chilies are added.

Indonesia: Indonesia is an archipelagic nation with various regional cuisines. Great dining establishments may be found in Medan, Sumatra, Yogyakarta, Semarang, Java, and Bali. The cuisine is diverse since the region spans more than 5,000 miles from east to west (as the crow flies) and includes more than 13,000 islands. Just a few of the delicious dishes available include beef rendang, barbecued fresh fish, grilled goat satay, creamy chicken curries, crispy suckling pig, and, of course, steaming vegetables doused in peanut sauce, known as gado gado, or gado2, which is sold on various foot carts.

Must-try dish: Nasi campur, a variety of dishes served with rice, maybe including a curry, an egg, some veggies, and a cake.

Laos: Due to the colonial era, Laos' two largest cities, the capital Vientiane and Luang Prabang, both have a wide variety of restaurants serving both traditional Lao food and sophisticated French cuisine. Laos has an indigenous cuisine; you may have to look harder than elsewhere. However, many of the country's most popular delicacies are adaptations from Thai, Vietnamese, and Chinese cuisines.

The culinary schools in Luang Prabang are well-known for emphasizing a local cuisine that is little known outside of its borders. Popular Lao dishes include steaming bowls of noodle soup sold on the side of the road, French baguettes stuffed with raw papaya and pate, and scorching hot salads served with the country's staple of sticky rice at restaurants.

Must-try dish: Larp, a salad of meat, such as chicken, hog, cow, buffalo, duck, or fish, with fresh vegetables and sticky rice on the side, and seasoned with lime, garlic, fish sauce, mint leaves, spring onions, and ground toasted rice.

Malaysia: Highlights of Malaysian cuisine, which reflects the diversity of its population and is a feast of South Asian, Chinese, Indonesian, and Malay delights, include the street food of Penang and the seafood of Kota Kinabalu. Like Thailand and Vietnam, having a bad meal in this country is difficult.

Look out for Indian restaurants, where sometimes hundreds of binaries may be heaped high with savory meals bursting with flavor and saffron rice. Freshly prepared one-plate portions of char kuay teow (oh, the oil!), sizzling bowls of laksa, and delectable chicken rice are available in hawker centers and on the street.

Must-try food Flat rice noodles known as char kuay teow are often stir-fried in hog fat at temperatures close to smoke point with soy sauce, red pepper flakes, shrimp paste, and typically some seafood and beansprouts. There are now as many variations as hawkers selling the food, but they all have one thing in common: they are all delicious.

Singapore: The national dishes of Singapore include chicken rice, laksa, and spicy mud crab (watch the price!). Singapore, a global city, excels in high-end fancypants restaurants and hawker centers serving basic needs, accommodating both ends of the financial spectrum. In this city-state, you may plan your day around your favorite foods: Roti prata and coffee to start the day, chicken rice from a hawker center for lunch, and a hand-crafted cocktail in a speakeasy to end it. In the evening, visit Chinatown for anything from Vietnamese pho to Szechuan beef.

A must-try food is chicken rice, which immigrants from Southern China first brought to Singapore and has since become national cuisine. The whole chicken is typically cooked in a ginger and garlic-flavored broth, although it may also be steamed or roasted today. Sliced chicken, rice cooked in herb broth, and a side of hot sauce are all served in one dish.

Thailand: Of course, we would go to Bangkok, the northern Thai towns of Chiang Mai, the southern Thai city of Krabi, and the northeastern Thai city of Ubon Ratchathani. Thai cuisine is known for its extreme heat, almost making you gasp for air.

If you want a more genuine experience, try to taste Thai cuisine elsewhere; sometimes, it's as simple as moving a few blocks away from the major tourist area to discover where the people eat. While curries vary from mild to explosive and sweet to sour, soups range from clear to deep crimson. You might spend a lifetime learning about the incredible range of sweets and desserts made in Thai kitchens, ranging from street food to royal cuisine.

Must-try food: Khao soi, a bowl of soft and crispy wheat noodles in a light coconut curry broth with pickled mustard greens, shallots, lime juice, and chilies on top. This dish is famous in Chiang Mai.

Vietnam: A abundance of good food is available in the Vietnamese trinity of Hanoi, Hue, and Saigon. Handmade fresh spring rolls loaded with rice vermicelli, a few cucumber slivers, maybe some shrimp, and fresh herbs are delectable. There is no typical bowl of pho; the traditional dishes bun bo Hue comes in a dizzying variety of regional variations! It is typical for sauces and fresh green herbs to be strewn over the cuisine. Similar to Thailand, the food is prepared fresh and on demand.

Must-try dishes While there are untold numbers of different pho, or noodle soup, varieties, envision a bowl of steaming, herbal broth with fresh flat rice noodles, maybe some meat, and green onions, along with whatever other herbs and sauces you'd want.

Local Favorites

Southeast Asia is a diversified area with a long culinary tradition. In this area of the globe, each nation offers regional delicacies and cuisines unique to that nation. Here are a few of the most popular regional dishes from various Southeast Asian countries:

Thailand: Pad Thai is a stir-fried rice noodle dish with shrimp, tofu, bean sprouts, and peanuts seasoned with tamarind sauce and lime. Using shrimp, galangal, lemongrass, lime leaves, and chilies, tom yum is a spicy and sour soup.

Green Curry: Thai basil, coconut milk, chilies, and other meats or vegetables make the creamy green curry.

Vietnam:

Pho: A tasty soup made with rice noodles, fresh herbs, thinly sliced meat or chicken, lime or chile, and other ingredients.

Banh Mi: Vietnamese sandwiches called banh mi have grilled pork, pickled veggies, cilantro, and mayonnaise, among other ingredients.

Fresh Spring Rolls: Rice paper spring rolls loaded with shrimp, pork, fresh herbs, and vegetables are served with a peanut dipping sauce.

Malaysia: Nasi lemak is a flavorful rice dish cooked with coconut milk that is served with sambal (hot chili sauce), fried anchovies, roasted peanuts, boiled eggs, and slices of cucumber.

Nasi Lemak: The spicy noodle soup known as laksa is made out of rice noodles, prawns, chicken that has been cut up into little pieces, bean sprouts, and a variety of herbs and spices.

Laksa: Satay is skewered and grilled marinated meat, often chicken or beef, served with a peanut dipping sauce.

Indonesia:

Nasi Goreng: With kecap manis (sweet soy sauce), shrimp paste, garlic, shallots, and a variety of toppings, including fried eggs, chicken, or shrimp crackers, nasi goreng is a savory fried rice dish.

Rendang is a spicy meat meal cooked slowly with various tasty spices and coconut milk until it is soft and delicious. It is often prepared using beef.

Gado-Gado: is a name for a mixed vegetable salad with a peanut sauce dressing, often containing components including blanched vegetables, tofu, tempeh, boiled eggs, and prawn crackers.

Philippines:

Adobo: A typical Filipino meal prepared of meat that has been marinated in vinegar, soy sauce, garlic, and spices before being cooked till tender (typically pig or chicken).

Lechon: A whole roasted pig with wonderful, crispy skin often offered for happy occasions.

Halo-Halo: Crushed ice, sweet beans, fruits, and jellies are just a few of the components used to make the refreshing dessert known as halo-halo. On top, there is leche flan and evaporated milk.

These are just a handful of the mouthwatering regional foods around Southeast Asia. Foodies will enjoy the area's rich tastes, fragrant spices, and unique culinary traditions.

A Street Food Guide

Here is a list of well-known cities in Southeast Asia with thriving street food traditions, coupled with a street food guide for those cities:

Bangkok, Thailand: Street food has a long tradition in Bangkok. Look into the hawkers on Sukhumvit Road or busy marketplaces like Yaowarat Road in Chinatown. Don't pass on popular local delicacies like pad Thai, som tam (papaya salad), mango sticky rice, and famous Thai curries.

Ho Chi Minh City, Vietnam: the streets are littered with various food stands. Visit the Ben

Thanh Market or Binh Tay Market to experience Vietnamese cuisine, including pho (noodle soup), banh mi (baguette sandwich), fresh spring rolls, and savory seafood dishes.

Penang, Malaysia: Penang is a gourmet haven with a culinary history inspired by Chinese, Indian, and Malay cuisines. Visit the hawker stalls along Gurney Drive or take a walk through busy George Town to sample well-known foods like char kway teow (stir-fried rice noodles), nasi lemak (coconut rice), and satay (grilled skewers).

Singapore: Singapore's hawker centers are well-known for their delectable cuisine. Visit Chinatown Complex, Maxwell Food Centre, or Lau Pa Sat to experience famous foods, including Hainanese chicken rice, chili crab, laksa (hot noodle soup), and roti prata (Indian flatbread with curry).

Yangon, Myanmar: To understand more about the history of street cuisine in Yangon, Myanmar, visit night markets like the Bogyoke

Aung San Market or 19th Street in Chinatown. Samosas, tea leaf salad, mohinga (rice noodle soup), and succulent grilled kebabs are classic. Keep the following in mind while eating

Southeast Asian street food:
- Look for busy booths with plenty of movement to preserve freshness.
- Verify the suppliers' standards of cleanliness and hygiene.
- Be careful about the degree of spice if you're not used to it.
- Keep hydrated by carrying bottled water with you.
- Have wet wipes or hand sanitizer on hand for hygienic reasons.

Although just a few well-known venues are included in this book, street food may be found all across Southeast Asia. Investigating the flavors and specialties on the streets is a great way to glimpse the diverse local culinary culture.

Vegetarian and Vegan Options

In recent years, Southeast Asia has seen an increase in the popularity of vegetarian and vegan options. The region offers a wide range of culinary options, and many traditional dishes may easily be modified to fit vegetarian and vegan diets. The following is a list of vegetarian and vegan options available in Southeast Asia:

Thailand: A wide variety of vegetarian and vegan dishes are available in Thai cuisine. For example, green curry and massaman curry may be prepared without meat by substituting tofu or vegetables. The popular noodle dish Pad Thai may also be prepared without fish sauce or eggs. Furthermore, Thailand offers stir-fried meals, fresh fruits, and vegetables suitable for vegetarians and vegans.

Vietnam: Vegetarian and vegan options are easy to find because of the availability of fresh herbs, vegetables, and rice noodles in Vietnamese cuisine. Tofu and vegetable broth may be used to make the traditional Vietnamese noodle soup pho. You may modify well-known dishes like spring rolls (goi cuon) and banh mi sandwiches using seitan, tofu, or tempeh as the protein source.

Malaysia: The many flavors and influences of Malaysian cuisine are well-known. Even though meat is often a key ingredient in many dishes, vegetarian and vegan options are also available. Instead of meat, tofu or tempeh may be used in the aromatic rice dish nasi lemak. Several vegetarian and vegan options are available in Malaysian cuisine with an Indian flavor, such as dosas and banana leaf rice.

Indonesia: Because of its long history of plant-based cuisine, Indonesia has a wide variety of vegetarian and vegan meals. A popular Indonesian dish, gado-gado, is made of tofu, tempeh, mixed vegetables, and peanut sauce. Adding vegetables and soy-based proteins may alter the fried rice dish Nasi Goreng. Additionally, Balinese cuisine has several vegetarian and vegan options, like tempeh satay and veggie curry.

Singapore: A multicultural city with a thriving culinary scene that offers a variety of vegetarian and vegan options. Many plant-based alternatives are available in hawker centers and food courts, from vegetable stir-fries to meals that look like meat. There are many options for vegetarian and vegan adaptations of the classic dishes from Chinese, Indian, and Malay cuisines.

Philippines: Although vegetarian and vegan options exist, most Filipino cuisine uses meat. A variety of tropical fruits and vegetables are available at local markets. It is possible to make dishes like vegetable adobo, which is often made with a pig, without using these components, and there are even plant-based variations of well-known Filipino sweets like halo-halo.

It's important to remember that while vegetarian and vegan options are becoming easier to find across Southeast Asia, it's still advisable to specify your dietary needs in detail when buying food to ensure there aren't any unmarked animal-based ingredients. Furthermore, traditional condiments or sauces often include a fish sauce or shrimp paste, so it's important to check with the restaurant staff or choose inherently plant-based foods.

Dining Etiquette

While dining manners vary throughout the many countries in Southeast Asia, certain general guidelines might help you navigate the region's cultural quirks. An overview of Southeast Asian dining manners is provided below:

Thailand: Using a spoon and fork instead of chopsticks is customary in Thailand. Food is put on the scoop with the help of the knife before being taken to the mouth. Some meals can be eaten with chopsticks. It's customary to hold off on starting to eat until the host requests it. At the table, sharing meals with others is also expected.

Vietnam: The proper way to eat in Vietnam is with chopsticks and a small bowl of rice. Use chopsticks to eat from communal plates while holding the rice bowl close to your mouth. It is customary to take little bites and chew thoroughly. It's polite to leave some food on your plate after eating to show that you're full.

Malaysia: When eating traditional Malay or Indian cuisine, Malaysians often use their right hand to eat. For convenience, many eateries also provide cutlery. Sharing plates set in the center of the table is customary while dining with guests. Instead of using your own equipment, take meals from communal dishes using the serving spoons or utensils provided.

Eating with the right hand is customary in Indonesia particularly when consuming traditional dishes like nasi goreng or sate. However, urban regions often utilize utensils. In Malaysia, it is allowed to share plates with others and take meals from communal dishes while using serving utensils.

Singapore: Due to the diversity of the country, proper dining manners may vary depending on the ethnic cuisine you're consuming. Generally speaking, it is polite to hold off on starting to eat until the host or the eldest guest has done so. Use the utensils provided; avoid using your hands unless it is customary for the specific cuisine.

Philippines: Using a spoon and fork while eating is customary in the Philippines. The scoop transfers food to the mouth while the knife is held in the left hand. It is polite to wait until the host or the oldest person has started eating before you start. Another common practice is sharing meals; taking a small amount of food at a time is customary.

It's important to remember that these are general guidelines since eating patterns might differ among different people within a country. In Southeast Asia, you observe and imitate local customs or your hosts while dining is customary. Being accepting, appreciative of the cuisine of the area, and showing gratitude for the meal will always be valued.

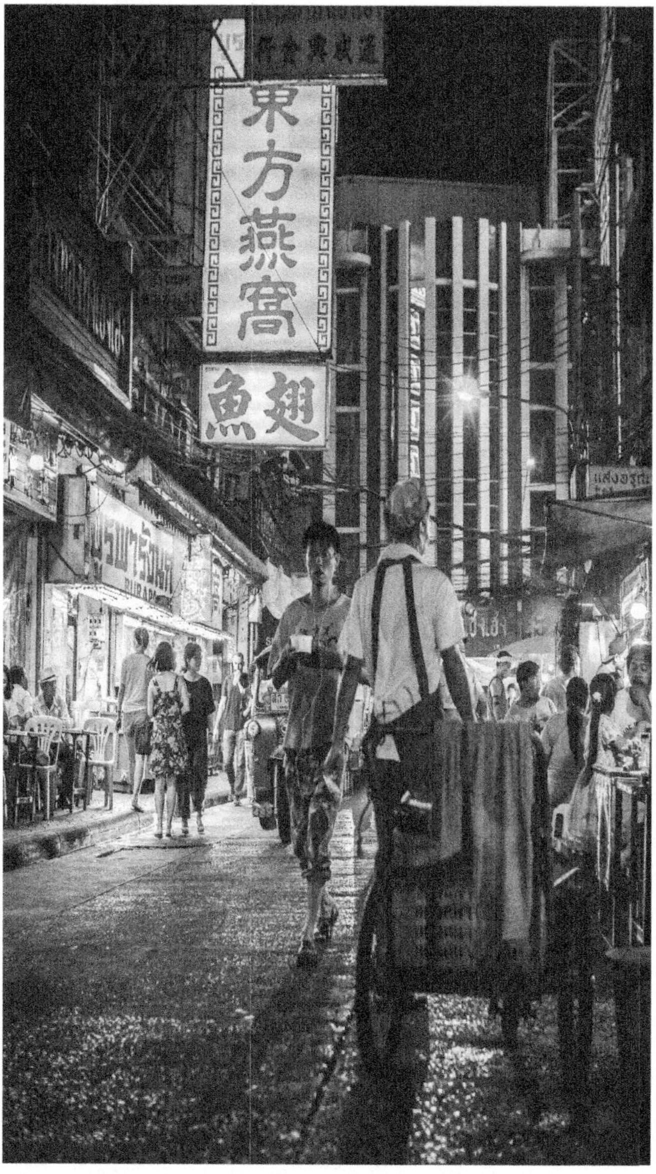
東方燕窩
魚翅

Chapter Seven

Cultural Insights

History and Heritage

The cultures and histories of Southeast Asia are many and diverse. Hunter-gatherers were the first people to live in the area, but small early governments had begun to emerge by the third century BCE. Several cultures, including Indian, Chinese, and Islamic, influenced these kingdoms.

Southeast Asia was significantly influenced by Indian culture. Indian culture was brought to the region by traders and missionaries, and it had a big impact on how Southeast Asian civilizations developed. The area's languages, religions, art, and architecture show signs of Indian influence.

Another notable cultural influence of Chinese culture in Southeast Asia. Chinese immigrants and locals have long made Southeast Asia their home, influencing the area's cuisine, holidays, and customs.

In the 14th century, Islam began to spread across Southeast Asia, and now it is the predominant religion in many parts of the area. The region's literature, art, and architecture all reflect the impact of Islam.

The history of Southeast Asia is also notable for several notable empires, including the Majapahit, Srivijaya, and Khmer dynasties. These empires were powerful and had a significant impact on the region.

Currently, Southeast Asia is a culturally varied region. There are many different ethnic groups in the area, each with its own unique culture and customs. Southeast Asia's diversity is one of the factors that makes it so fascinating and vibrant.

Religion and Beliefs

Here are some details about Southeast Asian faiths and ideologies:

With more than 42% of the population following Islam, it is the most widespread religion in Southeast Asia. Islam is the most common religion in Brunei, Indonesia, Malaysia, and the southern Philippines.

With almost 30% of the population following it, Buddhism is Southeast Asia's second most prevalent religion. Buddhism is the main religion of Thailand, Laos, Myanmar, and Cambodia.

Buddhism in Southeast Asia

With 15% of the population practicing it, Christianity ranks third among all the religions in Southeast Asia. Christianity is the most popular religion in the Philippines.

The Christianity of Southeast Asia

With around 5% of the population following it, Hinduism ranks as Southeast Asia's fourth most common religion. Hinduism is the most popular religion on the Indonesian island of Bali.

Southeast Asia contains a range of indigenous beliefs and traditions that are still followed in addition to these major religions. These beliefs often highlight the importance of spirits and ancestors and may include practices like divination, ancestor worship, and spirit mediumship.

In Southeast Asia, religion is often seen as important. It shapes people's moral and ethical behavior and gives them a sense of identity, belonging, and purpose. Religious practices and beliefs are often entwined with cultural norms, and they may be seen in many aspects of everyday life, such as celebrations, artwork, and architecture.

Here are a few examples of how religion is portrayed in Southeast Asia:

**Thaipusam, a Hindu event celebrated annually in Malaysia, honors the victory of good over evil. In remembrance of the occasion, devotees march by and pierce their bodies with hooks and skewers in a display of devotion.

Hindu mythological themes are portrayed by the traditional Javanese shadow puppet theater known as "The Wayang Kulit." The puppeteer controls the leather-made puppets from behind a screen.

UNESCO has listed the temples of Bagan in Myanmar as a World Heritage Site. The temples, which the Pagan Empire built in the 11th and 12th centuries, serve as a reminder of Buddhism's power and influence in Southeast Asia.

These are just a few examples of how religion and beliefs are expressed in Southeast Asia. The region has a strong and diverse religious heritage, making it an excellent place to learn about how people practice their faith.

Festivals and Celebrations

If a festival falls on your Southeast Asia backpacking trip, you're in luck! There are no festivals like the ones you've ever seen in this part of the world. Southeast Asian celebrations provide a unique cultural experience, from Thailand's greatest water fight (Songkran) to the horrifying body piercings and self-mutilations associated with the Hindu festival Thaipusam. Have you prepared your camera?

Thaipusam in Malaysia in January:

Every January, Southeast Asia celebrates Thaipusam, one of the most frightful celebrations in the region. Hindus all across the world commemorate the day in honor of Lord Murugan, the Hindu God of War and son of Shiva and Parvati.

One of the best places to see the event is in Kuala Lumpur, the multiethnic capital of Malaysia, where a yearly procession from the city to the renowned Batu Caves is held. The pilgrimage, which starts at midnight and finishes in the wee hours of the morning, attracts millions of travelers. They eventually make their way up the 272 steps to the cave entrance, where a large statue of Lord Murugan sits watch.

The "kavadi attain," also known as the "burden dance," is the celebration's most intensive element. As a demonstration of their devotion to Lord Murugan, devotees carry out difficult tasks like driving a huge chariot with metal hooks placed into their bodies or piercing their skin or lips with skewers. As they ascend to the caves, you will see several people wearing a heavy "kavadi" around their bodies. Some followers seem to be in a trance while performing their rituals, but the mood is strong and sometimes downright scary.

People start fasting and praying for Thaipusam 48 days before the actual day. You will see many couples carrying their infants up the steps to thank Lord Murugan for blessing them with a child the previous year and many people, especially new babies, having their heads shaved at this time.

Tet – Vietnam (February): The biggest holiday in the Vietnamese calendar is Tet or Vietnamese New Year. Tet Nguyen Dan, which translates to "The Feast of the First Morning of the First Day," is the holiday's official name. There are several similarities between the occasion and the concurrent Chinese New Year. Before Tet, many people would clean their homes and prepare special dishes like bamboo soup and sticky rice. Children get lucky red envelopes containing money, which is a particularly lucky time to pay off debts from the past, resolve conflicts from the past, start new endeavors, or create businesses.

If you're visiting Vietnam around this time, you'll see that the shops are bursting with mooncakes and red paper lanterns. People gather in the streets on the night of the full moon to make as much noise as possible with drums, fireworks, firecrackers, gongs, and whatever loud instruments they can find.

Similar to Chinese New Year, you'll see lion dances and people dancing while wearing masks. The objective is to ward off evil spirits that could be lurking around and prepared to invade the new year.

Nyepi - Bali (March): At this event, there won't be any music, clapping, or street laughter. In fact, you won't hear anything at all at this peculiar event in Bali! The Day of Silence, known in Bali as Nyepi, is observed annually on March 9. The occasion commemorating the 'Isakawarsa' New Year is exclusive to Bali's Hindu community.

Businesses, restaurants, clubs, and even Bali's International Airport are closed for a full 24 hours starting at 6 AM as people spend the day fasting or meditating. Besides a few security personnel who ensure that everyone abides by the current restrictions, Bali's often bustling streets are practically empty.

The festival aims to provide time for introspection, and if you're a traveler in Bali during Nyepi, you're also not exempt from the restrictions. Speaking inside your hotel room is advised, as no one is allowed on the street or the beach. For some people, a dreary day, but culturally a very fascinating day. Why not give yourself some time for introspection? The day after Nyepi, called Ngembak Geni, is the official Balinese New Year's Day, and it sees a resurgence of activity on the streets.

If you're lucky, you'll see many young single people participating in the 100-year-old "Kissing Ritual," or Omed Omedan, a ritual that serves as a kind of match-making for Bali's youthful population.

Songkran - Thailand (April): Can you imagine what a wonderful festival this would have been when you were a kid? So, let your inner child out as you prepare to participate in the biggest water fight ever! Around the middle of April, Thailand has three full days of wild and watery mayhem over the whole country. Anyone is protected from rain, and we do mean anyone. Young and old alike go to the streets armed with water cannons, super soakers, ice-cold water buckets, and even industrial hoses!

The Songkran Festival honors the Thai Buddhist New Year and has its roots in a much gentler custom. This process may still be in progress if you visit the temple on the morning of Songkran or a few days before the celebration. People may sprinkle water on each other and clean Buddhist statues as part of a symbolic "cleansing ritual" to welcome the New Year.

The purpose is to wash away the sins of the previous years and begin the new one with a clean slate, much as in many other parts of the world where people set New Year's resolutions and restart in the New Year. So cleanse your sins now!

Fortunately, the occurrence occurs during the hottest part of the year, making the water a welcome treat in Thailand's sweltering heat. One of the best places to see Songkran is Chiang Mai or Bangkok, where residents and tourists battle it out in the streets wearing colorful shirts. Similar celebrations in Laos, Cambodia, and Myanmar coincide with the Buddhist New Year.

Thailand's Phuket Vegetarian Festival takes place every October.

This event's name is rather misleading. It shows a group of vegetarians chowing down on healthy, fresh fruit and vegetables. Yes, the event attendees prepare for this occasion by consuming (only) vegetarian food. The main event is, however, a very other affair!

The festival, which has Taoist origins, is celebrated by Chinese communities across Southeast Asia, but nowhere is it more fervently observed than in Phuket, South Thailand, where around 35% of the population is Thai Chinese, descended from tin mine workers.

The festival, also known as the "Nine Emperor Gods Festival," is nine days long. It involves participants cutting themselves with swords, beach umbrellas, and other metal objects, as well as partial skinning, bloodletting, and other gruesome procedures! The activities are carried out in a trance-like state (always without anesthesia), and the scene is horrifying, drawing plenty of visitors and photographers each year. The actions are supposed to be a sign of reverence for the gods and ancestors. According to legend, the incident started when a group of Chinese opera artists arrived in town.

A devastating epidemic struck Phuket during the time, which caused many people to get ill and pass away. The Nine Emperor Gods had not been honored, one of the opera singers recognized. While the rest of the party refrained from consuming animal products, alcohol, or sensual pleasures, they first sent a troupe member to China to welcome the Gods to the town. The residents of Phuket commemorate the alleged disappearance of the illness each year with this lavish celebration.

Loi Krathong in Thailand (November):
One of the most beautiful festivals I've ever seen and one of my favorite Southeast Asian

holidays! On the evening of the November full moon, crowds gather in the streets to release paper lanterns into the sky (many holidays in Asia center on the full moon). (Krathong is the Thai word meaning lantern.)

Throwing their issues into the sky is said to alleviate their "dukkha," or misery. People float boats on rivers and lakes all around the country, along with lights. As a symbolic act of letting go of a portion of their past that they desire to leave behind, some people attach sections of hair, old photos, or messages to the boats before sending them sailing.

In Chiang Mai, the event is also referred to as the Yi Peng Lantern Festival. Mae Jo University is hosting a sizable lantern-releasing event a few days before Loi Krathong officially begins. Photography enthusiasts really must go to the event!

Naga Fire Ball Festival at Nong Khai, Thailand (November): One of the most mysterious festivals in Southeast Asia, the Naga Fireball Festival, is centered on an odd phenomenon that happens every November close to the Mekong River, which separates Laos from Thailand. Glowing red and orange fireballs are predicted to shoot hundreds of meters into the air from the river.

The 'Phaya Naga,' a serpent-like deity from Buddhist and Hindu mythology, is thought to reside in the Mekong River's depths and is credited for creating the balls. Naga sculptures may be found all around Thailand, including Nong Khai.

Numerous others think the thousands of people who claim to have witnessed the large balls of fire are a clever hoax. Some claim that the military firing tracer rounds bring the phenomenon into the air from the other side of the border. Others have hypothesized that a naturally volatile component in the water is to blame. Long-winded ruse or unresolved mystery? You must visit to verify for yourself!

Chapter Eight

Practical Information

Health and Safety

Numerous health and security problems are prevalent throughout Southeast Asia. One of the most pervasive issues is:

Road safety: In Southeast Asia, traffic accidents significantly cause fatalities and disabilities. With an estimated 316,000 road fatalities per year, it has one of the highest rates in the whole globe.

Waterborne diseases: Typhoid, cholera, and diarrhea are all waterborne diseases widespread in Southeast Asia. These illnesses may be brought on by drinking or eating contaminated food.

Vector-borne diseases:

Malaria, Zika, and dengue fever are widespread vector-borne diseases in Southeast Asia. Ticks, mosquitoes, and other insects are the carriers of these illnesses.

Malnutrition: is a serious issue in Southeast Asia, particularly for children. Numerous health issues, including slower growth, decreased cognitive development, and an increased risk of infection, may be brought on by malnutrition.

Unsafe workplaces: In Southeast Asia, workplace risks are a key factor in accidents and fatalities. Businesses often don't have basic safety precautions like machine guards, fire exits, and PPE.

In addition to these widespread health and safety problems, Southeast Asia also has country-specific issues. For instance, working in Indonesia carries a significant risk of exposure to dangerous chemicals. Landmine injuries are quite likely in Myanmar. In Cambodia, there is a considerable HIV/AIDS risk.

There are several things that may be done to enhance Southeast Asia's health and safety. These consist of:

Investing in infrastructure: such as roads, hospitals, and water treatment facilities, helps reduce the likelihood of traffic accidents, waterborne illnesses, and other health problems.

Strengthening health systems: Increasing access to healthcare and reducing the likelihood of preventable diseases are two advantages of improving health systems.

Raising awareness: Increasing people's understanding of health and safety issues may encourage them to take precautions for their families and safety.

By implementing these measures, Southeast Asia may make significant progress in enhancing the population's health and safety.

More safety advice for Southeast Asia is provided below:

Drink bottled water: Since Southeast Asia's tap water can be contaminated.

When driving or walking, be mindful of your surroundings and be on the lookout for any hazards.

Use insect repellent to protect yourself against illnesses spread by mosquitoes.

Get vaccinated: Obtain vaccinations for the diseases common in the region.

Get medical help as soon as possible: Seek medical attention when you feel sick.

Money-saving Tips

These financial saving suggestions are for Southeast Asia:

Stay in hostels or guesthouses: Hostels and guesthouses are great locations to save money on accommodation, so consider staying there. Sometimes, shared rooms are offered for only $5 per night.

Make your food: Dining out may be expensive in Southeast Asia. If you want to save money, prepare your meals. There are several affordable markets where you may get new things.

Take public transportation: In Southeast Asia, using the public transportation system is a great way to get about. Frequently, it costs substantially less than cabs or tuk-tuks.

Bargain: The practice of haggling is widespread throughout Southeast Asia. Never haggle for a reduced price while buying souvenirs or other products.

Use free activities: Southeast Asia offers many free things to do. For instance, you may go to museums, parks, and temples for free.

Travel during the off-season: If money is tight, consider going somewhere off-season. During this time, discounts are typically offered on lodging, travel, and activities.

Purchase a local SIM card: Doing so will allow you to use data and make calls for much less than you would pay with your international plan.

Be aware of your spending: Be careful with your money since it's simple to blow it while on vacation in Southeast Asia. Keep track of your spending to prevent going over your allotted amount.

Added advice is provided below:
- Pack light: Carry as little as possible since you'll save money on luggage costs.
- Please bring a reusable water bottle so you may avoid paying for bottled water and instead fill it up at water fountains.

Do your research: Before you go, find out how much lodging, food, and transportation will cost you in the places you wish to visit. This will assist you in setting up a budget and avoiding overspending.

Be flexible: Be adaptable since things don't always go as you want them to when you're traveling. If necessary, be ready to be adaptable to your plans and budget.

You may go to Southeast Asia affordably while still having fun by heeding this advice.

Connectivity and the Internet

The information that follows pertains to the Internet and connections in Southeast Asia:
With more than 400 million internet users, Southeast Asia has a high internet penetration rate.

The top 5 countries with the highest rates of internet adoption are:
- Hong Kong (85%)
- Thailand (82%)
- Bangkok (78%).
- Thailand (73%)
- Thailand (72%)

Mobile Internet: The most popular way to access the Internet in Southeast Asia is via mobile devices. More than 90% of local internet users use their mobile phones to access the Internet.

Fixed broadband: Although it is also available in Southeast Asia, fixed broadband internet is not used as often as mobile Internet.

Limited broadband internet in the region typically has a speed of 15 Mbps.

Challenges: There are certain obstacles to internet access in Southeast Asia. The high cost of internet access is one issue. The lack of infrastructure in rural areas is another problem.

Opportunities: Many opportunities have been presented by the Internet's rapid growth in Southeast Asia. For instance, the Internet has aided in promoting online education and e-commerce.

Overall, Southeast Asia is becoming more and more dependent on the Internet. Internet connectivity is expected to rise as the region grows significantly.

Here are some further details on internet availability in Southeast Asia:

5G: The most recent iteration of mobile internet technology is 5G. Compared to 4G, it is much faster and has lower latency. In Southeast Asia, 5G is still in its early stages of development, but in the next years, it is expected to grow rapidly.

Data centers: are places where data is processed and stored. For the internet economy, they are essential. Southeast Asia is home to many data centers, and it is expected that the region will play a major role in expanding data centers in the next years.

Cybersecurity: In Southeast Asia, this is a growing problem. The region is growing more vulnerable to hackers as it becomes more connected. The region's governments and businesses are working to improve cybersecurity, but more must be done.

Essential Phrases

Southeast Asia is a diverse region with a wide range of regional languages. However, a few basic phrases are useful to understand in any of the nearby countries. The following are a few of the crucial expressions:

Greetings:
Hello in Thai: Sawadee Krap,
- Namaste in Lao, Khmer, Burmese, and
- Konnichiwa in Vietnamese.
- Salutations (Malay)

Polite phrases:
- I'm grateful. Thai for "hop khun krap"
- The Vietnamese word for kamsahamnida
- Thank you (in Malay)
- I'm sorry. Thai: Kor tot krap
- Excuse me: Thai for "mai pen rai krap."

Basic inquiries:
- Khun khao khao khap, how are you? (Thai)

- Khun pood paasaa anggrit dai mai, do you speak English? (Thai)
- What is the cost: Bao nhiêu? (Vietnamese)
- In which bathroom are you located: Hong nam yoo tee nai? (Thai)

Useful words:
- I need aid: Thai for "khop khun chuay krap"
- I fail to comprehend: Thai: Mai khao jai krap
- Could you help me with this? Khao dai mai, Khun Chuay? (Thai)
- I'm unsure: Thai for "khop khun chuay krap."

These are just some essential terms you could need while exploring Southeast Asia. Learning a few phrases in the local tongue before you go is often a good idea since it will show that you appreciate the local way of life and make your excursions more enjoyable.

Here are some other suggestions for terms you should learn for Southeast Asia:

Begin with the fundamentals: Learn the most common salutations, polite expressions, and basic questions.

Consider using a phrasebook or online translator as a helpful resource for learning and translating new words into the native tongue.

Practice with native speakers: If you can interact with native speakers, practice your new vocabulary. This is a fantastic strategy for improving pronunciation and getting feedback on your development.

Don't be afraid to make mistakes since everyone does so while learning a new language. Don't let this stop you from using your unique terms in practice.

You may learn the fundamental phrases required for a successful trip to Southeast Asia with a little effort.

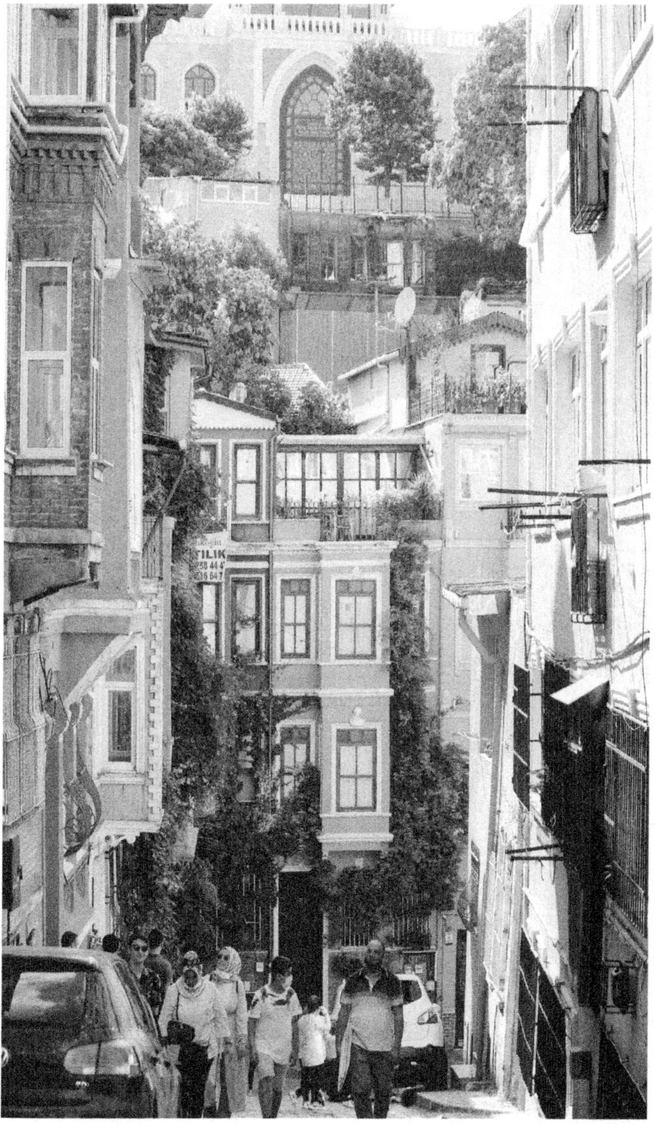

Conclusion

Recommended Reading

Here are some books for Southeast Asia that cover a variety of topics related to the history, culture, politics, and society of the area:

Anthony Reid's "A History of Southeast Asia: Critical Crossroads This book offers a thorough overview of Southeast Asian history from prehistoric times to the present. It discusses the many cultures of the area, colonialism, nationalism, and problems that Southeast Asian countries face now.

Southeast Asia: An Introductory History by Milton Osborne offers a straightforward yet helpful overview of Southeast Asian history. It provides a great beginning point for understanding the area's history since it contains important occasions, notable people, and regional dynamics.

"A Very Short Introduction to Southeast Asia by James R. Rush A concise and understandable introduction to Southeast Asia is provided in this little book. It covers the area's geography, history, religions, economics, and present problems, establishing the framework for further research.

The Singapore Story: Memoirs of Lee Kuan Yew" by Lee Kuan Yew Singapore's founding father, Lee Kuan Yew, shares his first-hand knowledge of the country's transformation from colonialism to independence and subsequent prosperity as a city-state. This memoir offers distinctive perspectives on Singapore's development and Lee's leadership.

George Orwell's fictional novel "Burmese Days": provides a glimpse into the colonial era in Burma (now Myanmar). It explores issues including racism, imperialism, and corruption while critically assessing the British colonial presence in Southeast Asia.

Indonesia: Exploring the Improbable Nation" by Elizabeth Pisani takes the reader on a fascinating tour through Indonesia, the largest archipelago country in the world. The author offers a thorough and detailed portrait of Indonesia's diversity, politics, culture, and challenges, as well as insights into the complex dynamics of the nation.

Vietnam: A New History" by Christopher E. Goscha, Following Vietnam's evolution from prehistoric times to the present, offers a fresh perspective on the country's past. It explores Vietnam's conflicts with other countries, the Vietnam War, and the nation's transformation.

The Philippine Experience: An Anthology was edited by Cynthia Nograles Lumbera. This collection brings together essays, stories, and poems that shed light on the Philippines' distinctive cultural heritage and socioeconomic struggles. It presents a variety of viewpoints on the country and its people.

Remember that many more excellent books on Southeast Asia are accessible; these are just a few recommendations. You could find other books that relate to your study topic depending on your particular interests.

Index

The Southeast Asia Index is a comprehensive rating system or statistic that assesses several aspects of the Southeast Asian region. It provides an overview of the countries in the region's economic, social, political, and environmental situations. While there isn't a single, well-recognized index for Southeast Asia, various rankings and indexes focus on multiple aspects of the region.

Economics Index: evaluate the competitiveness, growth, and performance of Southeast Asian countries. The GDP growth, inflation rate, trade balance, foreign direct investment, infrastructure development, and ease of doing business are often considered. The World Bank's "Doing Business" report and the World Economic Forum's Global Competitiveness Index are two indices that include Southeast Asian countries.

The Social Index: Social indices measure Southeast Asia's quality of life, human growth, and social well-being. Such concerns include efforts for social development, gender equality, access to basic utilities, poverty rates, wealth disparities, and education. One of the most significant indexes that cover countries in Southeast Asia is the Human Development Index of the United Nations Development Programme.

Environmental Index: Environmental indices evaluate Southeast Asia's ecological resilience, conservation efforts, and response to climate change. They include factors including air and water quality, biodiversity, deforestation rates, carbon emissions, renewable energy sources, and environmental laws. The World Wildlife Fund's Environmental Index and Yale University's Environmental Performance Index are global indexes that include Southeast Asian nations.

Political Index: Governance, political stability, democracy, the rule of law, and human rights are the main topics of political indices in Southeast Asian countries. They evaluate political freedoms, levels of corruption, press freedom, election processes, and the effectiveness of the administration. Both the **Democracy Index:** by the Economist Intelligence Unit and the Corruption Perceptions Index by Transparency International are well-known global rankings that cover nations in Southeast Asia. Remembering how different methods, data sources, and interpretative biases affect rankings and indexes is critical. Different scales may emerge from specific indices favoring certain factors over others. The political, economic, and social environments of Southeast Asian countries may also change over time, affecting their rankings in these categories. Consequently, examining the most current editions of several indexes for the most updated information about the region is preferable.

Printed in Great Britain
by Amazon